ONLY ONE THING
SPENDING TIME AT THE FEET OF JESUS

NOEL AND BARBARA BELL

WESTBOW
PRESS®
A DIVISION OF THOMAS NELSON
& ZONDERVAN

Cover artwork "Blue River", Simon Bull 2016, as a creative response to "Only One Thing"

Scripture taken from the New King James Version. Copyright © 1979, 1980, 1982 by Thomas Nelson, Inc. Used by permission. All rights reserved.

Scripture taken from *The Message*. Copyright 1993, 1994, 1995, 1996, 2000, 2001, 2002. Used by permission of NavPress Publishing Group.

Scripture quotations taken from the New American Standard Bible. Copyright 1960, 1962, 1963, 1968, 1971, 1972, 1973, 1975, 1977, 1995 by The Lockman Foundation used by permission.

Scripture quotations taken from the Amplified Bible (AMP). Copyright 1954, 1958, 1962, 1964, 1965, 1987 by the Lockman Foundation. Used by permission.

WestBow Press books may be ordered through booksellers or by contacting:

WestBow Press
A Division of Thomas Nelson & Zondervan
1663 Liberty Drive
Bloomington, IN 47403
www.westbowpress.com
1 (866) 928-1240

ISBN: 978-1-5127-5308-0 (sc)
ISBN: 978-1-5127-5309-7 (hc)
ISBN: 978-1-5127-5307-3 (e)

Library of Congress Control Number: 2016913383

Print information available on the last page.

WestBow Press rev. date: 10/5/2016

Only One Thing is based on Jesus's response to busy Martha.

He showed her that Mary had chosen the one essential thing: sitting at His feet to listen to His life-giving words (Luke 10:38–42).

FOREWORD

Günter Krallman, in his book *Mentoring for Mission: A Handbook on Leadership Principles Exemplified by Jesus Christ,*[1] coined a word: "with-ness." Krallman's inspiration came from scripture in Mark 3:14: "That they might be with Him." Jesus chose His disciples to be "with Him," that He might send them forth into the world.

Krallman emphasizes the importance of "with-ness" as preparation for "being sent," releasing an enabling grace that prepares the person, and the arena into which they are being sent, to accomplish the task set before them.

My first encounter of "with-ness" with Noel and Barbara Bell—and Jesus—was in a spiritual warfare conference convened by them at the Youth with a Mission (YWAM) facility in Goulburn, Australia, in 1979. I had not long returned to Australia after being absent for ten years, having left as a believer of eleven months, and resettling to start the Mission's Discipleship Training Programme.

The three-week encounter of waiting on God, walking in the light, and learning to fight the forces of darkness was a watershed of grace for me to launch into the next ten years of leading the work of YWAM in southeast Asia and Australia.

I found myself meeting again with Noel and Barbara in 1988, on a monthly basis, as a group of us gathered to be with one

---

[1] Günter Krallmann, *Mentoring for Mission: A Handbook on Leadership Principles Exemplified by Jesus Christ* (Atlanta: Authentic Media, 2003).

another and Jesus, to lay a spiritual foundation in prayer for the new Parliament House being built in Canberra. This led to what is now known as the National Gathering, a three-day event before the opening of the House that brought together around fifty thousand Christians (including denominational leaders) from across the nation to participate in laying a foundation of prayer and petition, and a prophetic call for the nation's future. Connections, strategies, encouragement, and ongoing relationships from that event will one day be fully revealed.

So it was without reservation that I responded positively to Noel and Barbara's passion to convene a gathering where we would come together to sit at the feet of Jesus.

To suggest today that we should meet non-stop for three weeks with no agenda—simply waiting on God—may cause raised eyebrows, but that is what we did. I remember distinctly how difficult it was for us to just be silent. At one point, it became easier, and we were completely quiet for about an hour. I was reminded of the scripture in Revelation 8:1, "There was silence in heaven for half an hour." It was not the silence of a vacuum, but heart-to-heart affection towards the Father, Son, and Holy Spirit as well as a deep sense of refreshing, comfort, and belonging.

Some people expressed frustration, thinking that there should be more, but we found that "with-ness" was enough. We were with the Father, Son, and Spirit, and we were with one another.

Jesus called His disciples to be *with* Him. So when we "do not know what to do," we now know what to do. As Jesus said, "Mary had the best idea" (Luke 10:42).

I wondered what this would lead to.

Now you can journey with Noel and Barbara, through four continents and numerous communities with diverse cultures, and experience for yourself this amazing documentation of prophetic words through the Holy Spirit to the gathered seekers. In reading, you will hear His voice. You will be drawn, as was each group, to set aside your presuppositions and personal agendas, to listen attentively to Jesus, and to find refreshing vitality to face the future. These recorded words, spoken to many gatherings, are timeless, and they bring comfort, encouragement, and correction.

Noel and Barbara have recorded a journey of being drawn to Jesus, but the greater story of what resulted in the lives of many others will be apparent in eternity.

Grace is poured out upon us as we acknowledge the worthiness of Him who spoke the worlds into existence, who became the Lamb of God, and who is now on the throne of God.

Come and let not your heart be troubled. If you believe in God, believe also in Jesus. Come and sit at His feet.

Tom Hallas
Director – Asia and Pacific
Youth with a Mission
July 2016

DEDICATION

This book is dedicated to Jesus.

He sowed the seed in our hearts to write this book, to encourage you to embark on the adventure of sitting at His feet. We are ever grateful to Jesus for His prayer:

"Righteous Father, though the world does not know You, I know You, and they know that You have sent Me. I have made You known to them, and will continue to make You known in order that the love You have for Me may be in them, and that I Myself may be in them" (John 17:25–26).

ACKNOWLEDGMENTS

We sincerely thank the many people who encouraged us to write this book and helped bring it to fruition.

The various times of sitting at the feet of Jesus were graciously hosted by leaders in Australia, Austria, United Kingdom, Finland, Germany, South Africa, USA, and Switzerland. These leaders included Ekkehard and Iris Höfig, David and Pauline Tidy, Ken and Ros Curry, Sally Fesperman, Graham Beggs, Antti and Helena Hämäläinen, and Werner and Regula Woiwode. We will always be grateful for their fellowship, participation, and wisdom (see the end of the book for their personal perspectives on the gatherings they organized).

Sue Hancock, who was our secretary at the inception of this journey, carried this book in her spirit from the outset and ensured that the draft text always reflected the heartbeat of Jesus. Her hours of typing and discussions, and her many other contributions to this book, have been a tremendous blessing to us. A case in point is the arrangements she made with her friend Simon Bull, an internationally awarded Christian artist, to create the original artwork for the book cover.

Judy Kay and Angela Hayles also played important roles in collating and typing our notes from the gatherings. Their efforts were a great help in assembling the material needed to produce the book. We also thank Judy Kay for her faithfulness in carrying this book in prayer from the earliest stages, as well as the larger group of friends who subsequently undergirded us in prayer while we were writing the book. Magda de Boer kindly assisted us with the scriptural references.

David Nathan guided us at a critical stage in deciding how best to present the rich lessons we learned while sitting at the feet of Jesus. His literary gifts and skills helped identify the merits of organizing the book in three parts to keep the focus on Jesus in a way that would appeal to a wide range of readers.

Our son, Johann, helped us rationalize and sequence the text and Barbara Coe and Catherine Hnidec edited the completed manuscript with great care.

Graphic design and IT advice were given in the final stages by Kelsley Nathan with much appreciation.

We also thank the staff at Westbow Press for their professional assistance in shepherding this book into print.

CONTENTS

INTRODUCTION

In a world where digital technology gives us unprecedented access to information, where the media constantly clamors for our attention, and where we can travel and amuse ourselves like never before, we run the great risk of failing to hear Jesus communicate with us. We can so easily miss spending our time in a way that will bring Jesus, and ourselves, the greatest joy.

In this book, we share with you how, together with other people, we learned to sit at the feet of Jesus to hear His voice. We have not discovered anything really new. Rather, by creating opportunities for the body of Christ to come to worship at His feet, we have rediscovered the age-old truth, lost by some churches, that "My sheep hear My voice, and I know them and they follow Me" (John 10:27 NKJV).

Jesus reaches out to us in many different ways: through creation, His Word, prophecies, dreams and visions; the Bible is a living, breathing documentary of a "God who at various times and in various ways spoke" (Hebrews 1:1). Indeed, Jesus has always been a passionate initiator of relationships. His heartbeat is that we, His people, would listen and draw closer, that we might know Him and be known by Him more intimately. It is the birthright of every believer to hear from God. Many people already hear Him speaking to them individually in their own quiet times, but this book emphasizes hearing His voice corporately.

The "words" that Jesus shared with us as we waited on Him do not add to or replace the Bible, nor do these prophetic words have that same level of authority. They are simply what we, and others who attended the gatherings described in this book, heard our Lord say through the gift of prophecy (Romans 12:6; 1 Corinthians 14:5) after worshiping Him and quieting ourselves so that He could surround us with His presence. These "words" reveal Jesus's strong desire to communicate with the pinnacle of His creation and assure us of His love.

Here, you will see the life and vitality with which Jesus shared His heart with those who set time aside to draw closer to Him. It is a story spanning decades over four continents. From raw beginnings came a montage of places and people who were hungry to be with Jesus and who had their hearts and minds transformed.

We invite you to join us in this discovery, chronicled in three parts:

Part 1 'Hearing One Voice' is a taste of the story of dedicating time just to be with Jesus. We all need to accurately hear His voice, and we trust that this account will spark in you a greater appetite to seek His presence.

Part 2 'Deep Calls to Deep' is a selection of the "words" we believe were given by the Holy Spirit through the gift of prophecy during the gatherings. As we have already stated, these "words" do not usurp scripture. We have referenced specific Bible verses in each of this section's pages, and we recommend you search the scriptures for yourself to enhance your understanding of the Lord and His great love.

Part 3 'Poised for More' outlines the key themes that emerged during these gatherings. They are especially relevant for a generation destined for increased revelation and fruitfulness in a rapidly changing world.

This is both His story and our story. We now invite you to make it your story.

Noel and Barbara Bell
July 2016

PART ONE

HEARING
ONE VOICE

1. THREE WEEKS ASIDE WITH JESUS

S ome years ago, Noel had a dream about a pleasant Mediterranean-style building with white walls and terracotta roof tiles. It had a large central courtyard with a cloistered colonnade around all four sides, leading to many rooms. In the center of the courtyard, Jesus sat quietly in a high-backed chair on a green lawn. The building represented His church, and the rooms spoke of the variety of ministries within the body of Christ. Each day, many of His servants entered the building and greeted Jesus with a cheery, "Good morning, Lord," before entering their rooms to work busily for Him. Meanwhile, Jesus waited for them to come and spend time with Him—to sit at His feet and listen to His words of life. While Jesus waited, He wept for His people who had overlooked their first need to spend time with Him.

The impact of this tragedy was very real. Jesus was deeply grieved, and our loss is consequently incalculable. How far have we strayed from coming to sit at Jesus's feet as our first priority every day? After all, He is the one who is building His church.

This brought to mind the early days when we met with others at our home for wonderful times of freedom in worship, joyfully sharing God's Word and praying together at the spontaneous leading of the Holy Spirit. It was during one of these nights that we first experienced coming to sit at Jesus's feet to listen and wait until He shared His heart with us. Through these times of vibrant worship, the Holy Spirit encouraged the group to enter into God's presence in the expectation that we would hear Him speak.

As leaders of Intercessors for Australia, a national prayer ministry, we organized prayer schools around the nation. Although our focus was on teaching about prayer, Jesus would sometimes take the initiative during a meeting, resulting in people surrendering their lives to Him through the gracious work of His Word and Spirit. Others were wonderfully baptized in the Holy Spirit, releasing them from their fears.

In 1991, we stopped off in Canberra to visit Tom and Di Hallas, leaders of Youth with a Mission (YWAM). Tom is a man who always has a focus on the big picture of God's purpose for His church's ministry to a lost world. Tom reminded us about the three weeks in 1979 that we spent with a cross section of the body of Christ at the YWAM base in the nearby town of Goulburn. We were set free from our rigid Christian attitudes before learning afresh the basic principles of spiritual warfare and intercession. Tom impressed upon us vital lessons on learning to hear His voice through times of worship and prayer.

We visited Canberra again in early 1992, which led to Tom suggesting we should set another three weeks aside with Jesus. "We have a responsibility to provide an opportunity for tomorrow's leaders to come aside to hear what Jesus wants to say to them regarding the times in which we now live," he said. Tom's words struck a chord: we yearned for a way to help Christian leaders draw closer to Jesus, allowing Him to speak directly into their lives. It is Jesus's words that give us life, strength, and purpose. This is what absorbed Mary's attention to the point of Martha's frustration. We must avoid the trap of being overwhelmed by Christian duty because it can rob us of opportunities to be still and hear the voice of Jesus.

With Tom's encouragement, we arranged for a broad cross section of leaders to gather in Canberra in August 1992, to spend three weeks with Jesus, to know Him better, and to learn how to walk in His purposes during the approaching new millennium. We invited several keynote speakers to lead each week. No-one was available except Johannes Facius, a leader of an international movement of intercessors. Johannes wanted to attend simply as a delegate because he had never done anything like this before. We then realized that Jesus did not want the gathering to be led by others. He wanted to be the sole focus.

Before going to Canberra we received an encouraging scripture: "Those who come He shall cause to take root in Jacob; Israel shall blossom and bud and fill the face of the world with fruit" (Isaiah 27:6). Although this word is a wonderful promise of God's end-time blessing for Israel, His own people, it also revealed God's intended purpose for the gathering: those who attended would become intimate with Jesus, and this intimacy would bountifully enrich His church in our day.

The following prophetic word revealed His strategy for the gathering:

> "As you worship Me, I will come amongst you and give you My Word to proclaim over the nation, a proclamation of My Word to push back the enemy's lines. It is not your crying to Me that will be the way I will lead you at this time, but the worshiping and extolling of My mighty name and the proclamation of your faith in My Word and My desire to move

in this land. As you worship Me, My presence will come amongst you and I will speak clearly to you and I will give you My Word to proclaim. This is My strategy, not the wisdom of man. You bless Me when you choose to come aside to worship Me and hear My voice. I delight in you and rejoice over you with joy; fear not! Be at rest in Me. I am with you."

How powerful this prophecy proved to be. More than ninety pastors, elders, and leaders of Christian ministries, including Australian aboriginal leaders, gathered in Canberra. We were supported by a group of intercessors who received a word expressing Jesus's heart's desire:

"My heart is broken by the indifference of My people. They call Me Lord by name, but they do not know Me. I have brought you here that you might learn to know Me. I have planned this gathering for some time. You'll be brought into a realm of My glory, and you'll never be the same again."

Before the first session in Canberra, our small leadership team anticipated receiving a word of guidance to share with the participants. However, that was not to be. Jesus remained silent. How vulnerable we were without an agenda. We had no alternative but to tell everyone that we had not received any specific guidance for the meeting. Instead, we simply encouraged the group to enter into a time of worship. Little did we know that we would be saying the same thing each day over the entire three weeks.

Jesus intended to reveal His heart to us step by step as we worshiped Him. Just imagine it: no program and no scheduled speakers. Many of the participants had never before waited for Him to speak to them nor allowed Him to take the initiative—something that was at the core of the early church as seen in the Book of Acts. This challenged us regarding the way we relate to Jesus personally and its implications for our lives and ministries. We were learning to see situations from His perspective and to discern the way that the Holy Spirit would lead us through God's Word and the varied gifts of the Spirit.

The first thing He revealed to us was our need to put down our "spiritual baggage": our strong theological views, past blessings, and even the ministries we had received. His aim was to set us free from our limited understanding. We were challenged by the following prophetic word:

> "I have chosen to call you together. Open your hearts so that I can speak to you, for now is the hour when I am calling My people from the four corners of the earth. I will raise them to a higher plane than they have experienced. For it is there that they shall join hands with Me, and stand to intercede, and set boundaries against the powers of darkness to release My people. I shall call you by name and draw you to Myself. Sanctify yourselves, for you are standing on holy ground, for this shall be a holy time. Set aside the things you have been involved in and consecrate yourselves. Stand before Me. This is a special time when I want to meet with you, when I shall speak My words to you."

As we worshiped together on the second morning, Jesus poured out His heart of love to draw us all closer:

> "I am jealous for your love. I would have you give your love to no other. My lifeblood was poured out for My body that you might glorify Me, for I am your Lord. You have labored long hours for Me. As a father works for his family, yet is separated from them, so you have been separated from Me. You long to love Me, but you are afraid to let Me love you with My strong bridegroom love. I long for your sweet fellowship."

This word was reinforced through a picture someone in the group received of a bride and groom, dressed in their bridal garments, entering the front door of their new home. All the bridegroom wanted to do was to pour out his love upon his bride. However, the bride, in her beautiful gown, wanted to express her love for him by cooking as well as washing and ironing his clothes. Meanwhile, he patiently waited for her in the bridal chamber.

What a graphic depiction of the church today. We need to let Jesus love us with His bridegroom intimacy instead of "doing things" for Him. Imagine what could be conceived by the Spirit of God for His church's eternal purposes if the basis was a strong marriage relationship with our Lord.

Something happened that day as the seed of His love was planted deeply into our hearts. We were in a womblike experience, waiting to give birth to something that God was yet to do. He covered us with His bridegroom love as we meditated on the

verses of deep intimacy revealed in the Song of Songs. This was confirmed by a word given through the Holy Spirit:

> "I have called you aside for a special purpose; I called you in days gone by but you were not listening. As I called Moses up onto Mt Sinai, I have called you into My presence that you would be silent before Me, that you would listen to My voice, that you would be intent on loving Me as I love you, for I am your Lord. Do you understand that you are the delight of My heart? Do you understand that there is a time for serving, a time for working together, there is a time for loving, for sleeping, for resting together—for Me to hold you in My arms?"

Our daily rhythm of spontaneous worship and prayer led us into new dimensions of adoration for Jesus. Our experience was not unlike Mary breaking open the alabaster flask, as our worship flowed like the fragrance of the costly perfume poured over Jesus's head. We learned to relate more intimately with Jesus. At times, we were prostrate in awe of His presence. One leader exclaimed, "Lord, I never knew it was so easy!" Later, he shared that he had always struggled to hear Jesus speak to him personally. How simple this became as the power of God's Word flowed through him and as we worshiped under the anointing of the Holy Spirit. There were times when Jesus spoke to us both individually and as a group. Through Mary's example, Jesus made it plain to us when He said, "Only one thing is necessary ... really only one!" (Luke 10:42). Learning to sit at Jesus's feet and listen to His words is essential for receiving His continuous flow of life.

It took some time before we all settled down to hear Jesus asking us to be quiet in His presence. At first, we could only manage ten minutes before someone would break the silence by sharing some personal blessing they were experiencing. Someone received a picture of us all climbing the rock face of a mountain. As we climbed, we looked back through the mist to see where we had left our baggage. On the summit, we entered a beautiful room bathed in golden light with a throne. We saw how God was leading us into times of deepening love, humility, and enjoyment of Himself and each other. We were being set free from our "Christian mind-sets"; it was a time of healing our wounds and allowing Jesus to draw us into a deeper bridal relationship.

Day by day, we were growing in grace, reflecting on what Jesus had already done through His priceless redemption and the power of His resurrection life. Creative gifts flowed spontaneously under the influence of the Holy Spirit. Someone played the violin and began to worship Jesus in old-time blues-fiddle style. A pastor's wife regained her gift of composing poetry; in a poem, she expressed the inner meaning and emotion about the cost of being His bride.

By the second week, we wondered how much more we could take in of the freshness and beauty of Jesus's ministry to us. One thing was becoming clear: He had started the process of remolding us into His likeness. We began to recognize that much of our work was done in our own strength, not at His initiative. We were learning what it means to die to self and to live as those "hidden with Christ in God" (Colossians 3:3), learning that Jesus literally is our life. We were at a breakthrough point as His healing balm began to work amongst us, opening our hearts to transparently share our innermost thoughts. The following comments from participants reveal something of the transformations that occurred:

> "Thanks for letting me sing. It's been a real healing for me to learn to speak from my heart. I'm here to get a transplant, to learn the language of Jesus's love."

> "In the past, I have been hurt so much that I have found it hard to truly love. Now that I have experienced Christ's love in a deeper way, it is easy to love with His love. I am learning to let God be God."

> "I have found a new security in the Lord. After being hesitant, I've given the leadership of my life back to God, and I know He will purify it."

We were challenged to come to grips with our past experiences—events that Jesus had allowed—to see how they could be used to lay sovereign foundations in our lives. We realized that each circumstance, whether good or bad, could become a source of strength instead of a handicap. We learned to accept His rule in every situation we encountered with true thankfulness. At this point, we received a very encouraging word:

> "I am coming to you as a servant, washing you with My tears, opening your eyes and ears, and putting something in your hearts which will endure. I am not finished with you yet. There is still so much more I want to tell you. All I ask of you is that you open your hearts to Me, and rest in Me, content to love Me, and

seek Me in the secret place of your heart. I will never leave you. I love you My children and My desire is to see you grow."

Instead of letting the Holy Spirit take the initiative, there was still the tendency to break our silence by expressing our thoughts with more scriptures, songs, and pictures. We were learning to be still and to rest in Him. Nevertheless, after enjoying days of His tender love and teaching, one morning, the group's prayers were sidetracked. We ran ahead of Him with strong prayers for the aboriginal people of Australia. How prone we are to allow our emotions to dictate our prayers, forgetting that we first need to receive Jesus's burden and His heart of love for this unique people.

Once we learned that without Jesus, we could do nothing of eternal value, we were better prepared to listen to Him speak. During a time of glorious worship, He spoke audibly through the Holy Spirit to Johannes, a gifted teacher, saying, "My people do not live in the fullness of what I have done" (see Colossians chapter 1: 17–19 and Ephesians chapter 3: 14–19). Johannes shared that Jesus wants us to live in the fullness of His love, which surpasses knowledge; the fullness of His victory for us over the power of sin; and the fullness of how He reconciled us with God the Father on the cross. We also need the fullness of the Holy Spirit's baptism, which has the power to make us one body. If we consistently lived in this measure of fullness, barriers in the church would come crashing down.

This understanding posed some searching questions regarding the quality of our love for Jesus and His church. Is our love

relationship with Him our first priority? How far have we entered into the full dimensions of Jesus's love? Have we withdrawn our love from anyone?

During the final week in Canberra, we grappled with the implications of all that Jesus shared with us. Where was all of this leading? Learning to come together simply to worship Jesus, waiting for Him to take the initiative, was very testing. We were not accustomed to following the Holy Spirit's leading for opportunities for Jesus to share His heart with people who are willing to listen to Him.

Carefully, lovingly, the true condition of our hearts, our insecurities, and the unbrokenness of our wills became apparent. We realized that we often see Jesus through our own needs instead of being available to draw others to Him. How we need to know the depth and poverty of self! Someone cried out in prayer as we sensed some of the pain He feels for His church in Australia:

> "Jesus, You have washed us, cleansed us, and beautified us through the shedding of Your blood. As our bridegroom, You have shown us Your strong love. You have revealed Your heart's desire for a people who will be truly Your own, yet we have stubbornly gone our own way. Forgive us for our foolishness in not responding to Your heart's cry. Help us to be totally Yours alone. Please take the initiative and draw us closer to You with Your deep love, which will radically change us into Your likeness."

That prayer reminded us that we are called to reflect the life and character of Jesus in our communities. The eight qualities of the Beatitudes should be our measuring stick. We heard His heart cry for us, His church, to willingly yield and yield again.

Isaiah 55:1 sums up the time together in Canberra: "Ho! Everyone who thirsts, come to the waters!" Jesus was deeply moved as we worshiped and waited on Him. The words He shared with us from His heart drew us into a deeper covenant relationship with Him. As we prepared to go home, we sensed that the Lord had gone ahead, speaking to us through several verses of this chapter of Isaiah and encouraging us to remember the following principles:

- God commits to guide us in His ways as we willingly come to sit at Jesus's feet to worship, to wait, and to listen to Him speak.
- Do what He does and speak what He says, being constantly sensitive to the Holy Spirit's leading to walk in His ways.
- Hunger and thirst after an intimate relationship with Jesus as we yield to His Spirit and feed on the rich manna of His written Word.
- Be content to wait until He speaks and guides when we do not know what to do or say.

Throughout those three weeks, we experienced a new level of being in the presence of God. The rich times of worship opened up the way for Jesus to bring fresh light and understanding to our hearts. In turn, this ignited powerful prayers guided by the Holy Spirit. Jesus visited us to share His words of life and

express His longing for an intimate love relationship with each one of us. Our hearts burned within us while He spoke.

Gently, patiently, and with quiet determination, we were unraveled from our set Christian lifestyles. The words Jesus sowed in our hearts He promised to water to produce good fruit. We saw that we can trust Him in all circumstances of our lives and rest in confidence that He has everything in His hands as the days unfold. He will bring His purposes to pass through us as we reflect His character in thought, word, and deed. All that Jesus asks is our trust, obedience, and a heart overflowing with love towards Him. It is only as we behold the face of the Lord, and come to understand His burdens for the church and the world, that we can effectively minister to others. We learned that our first priority should be to wait until we hear Jesus speak. Only then, under the Holy Spirit's anointing, are we free to share God's Word with others. When we live this way, our fruitfulness for His Kingdom is boundless.

On returning home to Germany, Johannes confessed that he would never be the same again. Sitting at the feet of Jesus had refocused his life and his whole way of thinking. He discovered that true discernment only comes when it is perceived through Jesus's heart. As Jesus said, "It is the Spirit who gives life, the flesh profits nothing. The words that I speak to you are spirit, and they are life" (John 6:63).

2. LEARNING TO FOLLOW HIS LEADING

T he following year, Johannes joined us again to sit at the feet of Jesus at three different locations in Australia. As Johannes was en route from Germany, he asked the Lord, "Why am I going to the other side of the world when there are so many opportunities for ministry in Eastern Europe and Israel? What is the purpose of needing to be silent and sitting at Your feet?" Jesus quietly responded, "Are you not willing to 'waste' three weeks in a year on Me? This is My appointed way of changing you more into My likeness. I am going to teach you to do nothing, in a meaningful way, while you are in Australia."

Those three gatherings were the next step in our learning process. Jesus challenged us to consecrate ourselves to Him wholeheartedly. He wanted to transform us into living sacrifices that would manifest His life to the world and bear much fruit for His kingdom.

The Holy Spirit anointed Johannes to open up God's Word to teach us to be ministers of the Spirit, to be liberated from the letter of the law, and to be purified by His refining fire. This was both an encouragement and an admonishment to us:

> "You insist on lighting fires with your own box of matches—your own good works. Give Me your matches so that every fire that is lit in the future is My fire, with My love at its center. Come into the Holy of Holies, come and rest at My knee. My yoke is not heavy; it is a bond of love with which I tie you to

Myself. Come to Me; let Me love you and show you how to love, for I am love. Just allow My love to wash away all your fears, hurts, and anxieties. Your future is in My Hands. Come to Me, and I will teach you how to let the light of My love shine through you. Do not fear, for My love is stronger than all the powers of darkness."

A Time of Confession

There were times when Jesus invited each one in the group to come aside and focus solely on Him. Noel asked, "Lord, what is the next spiritual challenge that you have for me?" He responded, "Are not you satisfied just to be with Me?" revealing Noel's mind-set. Jesus was not asking for service; He was asking for intimate, one-on-one fellowship.

Here are a few examples of individual responses to being with Jesus by members of the group:

> "Forgive us, Lord, that we have given more importance to this life than to the transcending life we have in You eternally. Teach us not to cling to this life but be ready to be taken into the fullness of Your love."

> "I am convicted by my preoccupation of relating to people on a 'ministry basis.' I have not spent meaningful time in getting to know and love my brothers and sisters in the Lord, or learned to respond with the love, joy, uniqueness, and delight

with which Jesus loves them. Jesus, please teach me to walk and live this way."

"Lord, forgive me for a love so shallow that it wants its own way, so impure that it doesn't know what to do next. How, Jesus, did I ever think that I could walk through the days ahead hoping to rest in Your presence, embalmed in Your love, secure and satisfied by You without being radiantly caught up in the fullness of Your being?"

"In drawing near to Jesus, I need to allow all my senses to be filled with Him, to gaze upon Him, to hear Him through His Word in my inward ear, to savor His fragrance, to touch Him in faith, and to taste the power of His resurrection life."

One pastor summed up the time we had spent with Jesus:

"The Lord has done a life-changing work in us. As we go from here, we need to apply our wills to the things we have learned so that we will be fruitful in the days ahead. So let Jesus alone be the prime mover of our motives. He will teach us how to wait upon Him, and in His time, show us His glory. Yes, He will visit us."

During the last meeting, Jesus drew our attention to Isaiah 48:6 and 17, declaring in part, "I have made you to hear new things, even hidden things you did not know. I am the Lord your God who teaches you to profit, who leads you by the way you should go."

New Directions

Upon returning home, we enjoyed reflecting on all that Jesus revealed to us. We decided not to hold any further gatherings of sitting at the feet of Jesus for fear of "manufacturing a ministry." As we were praying one morning, Jesus clearly revealed to us that "it is finished." Our response was, "Yes, Jesus, your work on the cross is indeed gloriously finished." This was not His point. Rather, He was showing us that we were to lay down the leadership of Intercessors for Australia.

As we broke this news to our secretary, Sue Hancock, she was not surprised. She had earlier received a guiding word from Jesus for us: "This is not a period of 'death,' but a period of release. The new thing I have for you will be greater than before. It will be on a different level—much more in prayer and worship. You will be released to minister more in My Spirit and see Me moving in a new way in the hearts of My people in Australia and in other nations.'

During this time, Noel's cardiologist became more concerned about his heart condition and recommended that Noel retire from an active life to live quietly at home and do a bit of gardening. This did not line up with the word that Sue had received. We were greatly encouraged when a group of African leaders, who had heard about Noel's heart condition, surrounded him during a meeting of intercessors in South Africa, praying powerfully as they leaned on God's faithfulness for the restoration of his health so that he could complete his calling. It was a wonderful and rich expression of brotherly concern.

Hearing One Voice

In 1993, things crystalized for us when we led a team representing the Pacific Oceania zone at a Gideon's Army Gathering of three hundred intercessors held in South Korea. After the last meeting, our team prayed together for God's guidance for each of our futures. One brother shared a picture regarding the days ahead for us as a couple. He saw us as two trees covered with autumn leaves. As each leaf fell onto the forest floor, a tender new plant grew up. Looking back, we can see how new life sprouted forth from hungry ones from many nations as they sat at the feet of Jesus.

Everything fell into place through Jesus's guidance. It took a few months to wind up the intercession ministry and hand it over to the next generation. The period of release prophesied earlier opened up when we received an invitation to spend time with others on the island of Åland, located between Finland and Sweden.

Our hosts, Antti and Helena, had stepped out in faith to buy an old timber schoolhouse on the island set among fir trees and moss-dappled rocks, which they renovated into a prayer center with their living quarters attached. People attending the prayer-center gathering stayed in summer cottages in nearby coves along the shore. We had heard that the Finns were a dour lot because they had to spend a good deal of the year living in subzero temperatures. This was far from the truth—they crammed into the prayer center, hungry and thirsty to meet with Jesus. Before the first session started, we received the following word:

"Take things quietly today. This is not a day for rollicking and fun. I have some serious business I must do among you all. It will take real sensitivity on your part to know and see what I am doing in each life. It is fine to praise and worship Me—I rejoice in this—but there are a number among you who do not know what it is to really praise and worship Me. I want to speak to them and reveal Myself to them in a new way. So take things quietly until you see that I have touched them and that their need for My love to be showered upon them has been met."

Over the next six days, many lives were transformed by the ministry of the Holy Spirit and the life-giving power of God's Word.

Other Doors Begin to Open

After Finland, we visited a church in Nuremberg, Germany, where the pastor and his wife were recovering from an extraordinary injustice through a threat of being jailed by the city authorities. Some months after their harrowing time, we had the opportunity to encourage them to come aside with their leadership team for a time of spiritual refreshment. As we met together in the Bavarian countryside at Schlossau, it was not long before the Holy Spirit's ministry of liberty and freedom began to heal and restore the group, renewing their joy and confidence in Jesus's care and guidance. Through this opportunity, other doors were opened to meet with believers in several locations in Germany over a number of years. Each gathering was uniquely tailor-made by the Lord.

Next, David and Pauline Tidy invited us to spend time sitting at Jesus's feet at Ashburnham Place in Sussex, England. This

ancestral property was gifted to a Christian trust in 1960 as a haven of peace and spiritual refreshing for the body of Christ in Britain. Its parklike setting of two hundred acres included three lakes and many mature oak trees. Our gatherings were held in a prayer center, originally built as a coach house, surrounded by staff cottages around a cobbled courtyard. These gatherings continued for seven consecutive years, providing an orderly flow of worship and a wealth of teaching to the church to walk in the fullness of her inheritance.

At these different venues, the story was the same as people confessed how they needed to stop in their busy lives to spend time with Jesus, knowing they were like Martha but longing to be like Mary. They understood that time was needed to wait for His words of life to guide them. We saw people being set totally free from past bondages as they refocused their lives on Jesus.

As guests in these nations, we worked together as a team with the local leadership. We were all learning to allow the Holy Spirit to take the initiative for each gathering. As you can imagine, this was much like walking on water. Oh, we learned so much. Only Jesus can minister fruitfully to a gathering of His people— each one with his or her unique personality, background, and expectations. It is the Holy Spirit who draws us together in oneness in our worship and adoration of Jesus.

We were challenged to ask, "Why do we spend so much time seeking intellectual satisfaction over the Word of God when the Holy Spirit is waiting to lead us into the Lord's presence through worship and to bring His Word alive?" How Jesus longs to share

His heart with us across the whole spectrum of His living Word. We have little concept of the joy we bring to Jesus when we give Him the opportunity of drawing us closer to Himself.

We need to ask ourselves many questions. Are we truly living in the freedom that Jesus has won for us on the cross? Do we really know what He means when He says to us, "If the Son has set you free, you shall be free indeed?" (John 8:36). Have we come to the place where He truly lives freely in each one of us, revealing more of His beauty and majesty so that He can do whatever He pleases through us? We were greatly helped by the Holy Spirit to grasp a deeper measure of the breadth and power of Jesus's earthly ministry and His glory. We learned that the degree to which we have the freedom and the authority to minister to others in the power of Jesus's resurrection life is related to the degree that we have laid down our own lives to serve Him. When Jesus has unhindered access, He is free to do whatever He desires through us (see Luke 14:26–27).

Jesus's Guidance

Over the years, we spent time daily studying the words of Jesus in the four gospels. Later, we realized that this was important preparation in leading people to come and sit at Jesus's feet. This trained us to be ready to hear His voice at all times. Jesus prepared us in four different ways:– before leaving home, upon our arrival in a nation, prior to a gathering as a leadership team, and during a gathering. The Holy Spirit also gave us some final words of instruction at the conclusion of several gatherings.

Before Leaving Home

During our times of worship and waiting on Jesus at home, He would often encourage us personally with guiding words. These words became a source of continuing strength for us. It is a joy to share some of them with you:

"Wait to hear My voice before you speak. There are many things I want you to say and do while you are away, but they must all be done and said in context with My Word.

Otherwise, they have no power, no profit, and no long-standing blessing. So learn to wait until you hear My voice before you launch out into all I have prepared for you both. You need not strive. Let Me do the talking and the ministry. My people know Me and understand Me clearly when I speak to them. Go as My instruments to impart My life to all to whom I send you; I am with you."

"I am sending you to new places, places that cannot stand in their own strength, places that are not accustomed to hearing My voice. Do not take with you tools to repair the works that have been done by others. See with the eye of the eagle, understand with the heart of the deer, and walk as one clothed with My righteousness. I have many things to share with people you will meet, but they cannot hear unless they open their hearts first. Your part is to walk before Me daily in quietness of spirit until I give you the word to speak. Do not be foolish and run ahead of Me. Wait, wait; it will come, My Word anointed by My Spirit to break open the strongholds that have held them captive. Go in peace, go in My grace and My strength. Yes, with My hope and My hand to guide you and to keep you."

Jesus had earlier emphasized that our own lives must be a demonstration of the fellowship and likeness of Christ through the Holy Spirit, who waits to maintain in us a life that continually abides in Him. One year, the Lord encouraged us, saying:

"Go with the purity of My Word in your mouth, reflected by the purity of your life in Me, to share with My people the purity of life they have in Me."

He specifically gave us the following scripture to share with all the groups we were visiting:

"Since you have purified your souls in obeying the truth through the Spirit in sincere love of the brethren, love one another fervently with a pure heart having been born again, not of corruptible seed but incorruptible through the Word of God which lives and abides forever" (1 Peter 1:22 and 23).

Upon Arriving in a Nation

We usually took a few days of rest to wait on the Lord in a quiet location before meeting with the local leaders. Jesus would help us prepare our hearts with guiding words:

"Take it easy, take it slowly, take it quietly. I have many things I want to say and do among My people. But I cannot bestow My riches on My people while they cannot receive them. Many are idle, slow to respond to the leading of My Spirit, unaware of their condition. They lack a contrite spirit and a sense of hopelessness about the things of the world. They still cling to the security of what they have inherited on this earth. They have no heavenly perspective. Where do I begin to change them, unless it is through poverty of spirit, soul, and body? Would you join Me in this healing process that I want to bring to pass in their midst this week? Will you lay down all you know and follow Me as I minister to them and take the lead from Me? It is not easy for you, I know. Will you trust Me to show you a new way, a richer way, a surer way to follow Me than you have known in the past? If you are willing, I can begin to work and move from person to person, healing, encouraging, and drawing them closer to Me, blessing them. Let's begin this together" (Ashburnham Place, United Kingdom).

"Do not be disturbed. I have all things in hand; otherwise, why would I bring you away with this group? Keep calm and be at peace during the whole week while I work in people's hearts. You will discover many new things about yourselves that have been hidden until now. Come each day and separate yourselves to Me to receive My instructions for the day. Do not take lightly the things I put on your hearts. Do not carry them as burdens either. Talk to Me often. I will open up further understanding for you. I remind you again that you must leave everything in My hands. Rejoice that I am sending you to be with this group because they represent much of what is going on in My church in Germany. Above all else, be at peace, for I am with you" (Schloss Craheim, Germany).

Prior to the Beginning of a Gathering

As the leadership team met before the first meeting, we took the opportunity to recall some of the points that we had learned previously while sitting at the feet of Jesus:

- If we want to come and sit at Jesus's feet, we should be open and ready to be changed and to be set free from our own conceptions and free from any bondage; otherwise, we are not able to draw nearer to Jesus.
- Our approach to worship is very important. We come to worship Jesus, but worship itself is not the focus. We worship to be led into His presence.
- Our gatherings should be Christ-centered. They should not be ministry-centered, where the focus is on us.
- We need to lean on God's Word more and more, to accept His presence as a reality, and to not depend on our "feelings" of His presence.
- It is essential to set the Lord always before us during the whole day and not be sidetracked by other issues.

On a number of other occasions, Jesus encouraged the team to leave everything in His hands in teaching His people how to hear His voice:

"I identify with My people's needs. I am breaking chains and setting captives free. I am pouring out My light upon them. Do not be discouraged if you think nothing is happening. I am touching them deeply in their hearts, so deep they do not speak about it. Weeping will come upon some—weeping that brings freedom and release, and identification with the hearts of their brothers and sisters. Be patient; be at peace. You will see the blooming of new flowers in many lives for My kingdom's sake. What I am asking you to do is important. Do it My way. Above all, know that I come with the fullness of My life amongst you" (Hubmersberg, Germany).

"I have gathered My people here for a purpose to bring them into a new relationship with Me. It is My heart's desire to draw them closer to Me. Please be very sensitive to My Spirit. I want to sow new seeds in their hearts and fresh revelation about who I am. I want to speak to each one personally and gather them in My arms. Be patient with Me. I want to gather them as a hen gathers her chickens. There are many lonely ones here. I want to draw them closer to Me. Be understanding and patient so that I may work freely in their hearts at this time." (Åland, Finland).

"I want you to make straight paths before Me as you go to meet with your brothers and sisters. Do not hesitate to be bold with My boldness. I want to bring much joy to My people—much laughter, much blessing. I want to restore many hearts. I want to set others free. Be careful, be gentle, be humble, but most of all—be My loving, obedient servants. Have no fears. As you gather, My anointing will be upon you, and I will speak to lead you and guide you day by day" (Amden, Switzerland).

During a Gathering

There were times when Jesus shared a specific word with the leadership team during a gathering, reminding us of His desire to bring radical changes in the lives of His people:

"You take pride in the things you do for Me. Why do you do that? Because it is a substitute for knowing Me. You can know Me as My first disciples did—with all their faults. You can walk and talk with Me as they did, but you have an advantage over them because you have My Spirit within you. Do not substitute your Christian activity for the reality of truly knowing Me. Lay it all down and learn to simply *be* with Me without any conditions, without any striving to know Me. I am who I AM. Is not that sufficient? Learn to let it all go. Simply come to Me as you are, and we will commune together very naturally each day, Spirit to spirit. I will do the rest. I will take the initiative when it is necessary. Until then, be content to be with Me. Either I am your Lord, Master, and friend or I am not. You need to decide. Let Me encourage you to learn to

let go of everything. My Spirit will teach you how to do this. Be very, very sensitive to Me, and soon we will be moving together in such sweet fellowship, yes, ultimately for My Kingdom's sake" (Franklin, North Carolina, United States).

"Many people come to My throne; they come in droves, and they pay homage to Me, but they do not know Me, and they do not know My Spirit. It grieves My heart. I am waiting for openings, and I am waiting for opportunity, but most of all, I am waiting for a church that will listen to My still, small voice. When I speak, they will know it is Me. Will you help Me? Yes, you can. You can help Me by being willing to listen. I will teach you to follow My Spirit. It is simple, really. It is so simple, but only when your hearts are uncluttered with the busy-ness of your Christian lives. Will you help Me that I might help you? Will you?" (Ashburnham Place, United Kingdom).

"I have brought you into close fellowship for a purpose—because My people are going to cry out in the days ahead for places of shelter where they can meet with Me. This is what I am calling you to do for My people—to prepare a way for them. It is a great work that I am giving you to do. Do not despise it and do not neglect it. Carry on with what I have given you to do, and in time, you will see much fruit. I rejoice over you. Yes, I, your Lord, rejoice over you" (Amden, Switzerland).

"I have patterns and I have projects, but I do not bring these to you. This is not the way I will lead you to walk. This is not the ordinary way I am leading you. This is a costly way, costly and precious—a way of silence, a way of solitude, a way of making My own character known to My people. Most do not understand Me. They walk in the light I give them and rejoice, but they know nothing of My sufferings. I have kept My sufferings from them because they are children. Now is the time to bring maturity forth. It is costly, but the fruit is rich and beautiful. As you gather together to be with Me at this time, be sensitive to My Holy Spirit. Do not plan what you will do or say. I am drawing you closer to Myself, that I might reveal more of My heart to prepare My people for My return. They have tasted of Me, and the taste is beautiful and sweet. There is also the taste of bitterness and suffering that brings forth My life gloriously. I have new things to say to you all, so have ears to hear and make a way for My Spirit. Each day you are together is precious and important. Do not waste it on trivia. Let Me lead you and take you through the day. You will understand what I am saying to you for the strengthening of My people in the days to come" (Hubmersberg, Germany).

The words of direction to the leadership team usually occurred once we set our hearts to worship Jesus in song and through spontaneous expressions of our love for Him. The flow of His life was so apparent among us. For our part, we were growing in obedience to "come unto Him" (Matthew 11:28) and to give Jesus opportunities to minister to us in a personal way.

Final Words to a Group

Here are some examples of expressions of Jesus's heart to various groups at the conclusion of their gatherings to encourage and guide us all before we departed:

> "I have spoken to each one of your hearts, and I have drawn you closer to Me. You have tasted the sweetness of My Spirit and My love. Now I send you back to where you came from. You are changed. I have made many things new and fresh within you. You knew them before, but now I am going to pour out the fullness of My love into your hearts so that My love is poured out in turn into the hearts of the difficult, the lonely, and the brokenhearted. Draw close to Me each day, and we will be in sweet communion together. I have done a new thing in your hearts" (Niedenstein, Germany).

> "I have walked among you. I have touched you. I have given you My words of life. Strengthen the body of Christ back at home because I am equipping you for this purpose. All I have done in you, do unto others because My desire is for My whole body. Let My light shine forth and let the wind of My Spirit blow, as I have given it to you this week. Will you be My ambassadors so that My bride may prepare herself? Go and let Me breathe upon others so that they may

know My heart of love for them. You did not choose Me; I have chosen to speak to you (John 15:16). What you have received I will never take from you. I do not call you My servants, but My friends. I have brought you here to hear My words. They are words from My Father, and they are yours forever" (Åland, Finland).

He reminded us that "though our outer nature is wasting away, our inner nature is being renewed every day, as our light momentary afflictions prepare for us an eternal weight of glory beyond all comparison" (2 Corinthians 4:16–18). Spontaneously, people responded that they should learn to view their afflictions from an eternal perspective, allowing the Lord to draw them aside and preparing them for the times ahead:

> "As I send you home, you go with My peace upon you. Yes, storms will come and winds will blow against you. You will stand, and stand, and stand again because I have put something new in you. It is a deep, deep love. I bought this love for you that you might have it. It is sufficient for every situation, and more than that, you will pour it out upon others. Even as I touched you this week, you will touch others. Be ready for My voice to speak and show you what to do. You will know it is Me and not yourself as it will be bathed in My love. I love you" (Amden, Switzerland).

Sometimes, we received a sobering word:

> "The days are coming when you will be gathering together like this, but it will be in secret because

they are looking for you to put you in prison. It will be costly when you gather together, but I will be in your midst. I will guide you and lead you. They will be glorious days, and I will move in power as you have never seen before. Now is the time for you to prepare your hearts. They will be so entwined with My heart that you will understand even before I speak. It is so necessary that you draw close to Me in these days. Oh, My children, your gathering together here gives Me great joy. Continue to do this, as there is still much work to do" (Türmberg, Germany).

These examples illustrate our need to be continually aware of His presence, ready to hear from Him; oh, how we need to nurture our personal worship of Jesus under the Holy Spirit's anointing.

3. TIMES OF SHARING

O ver the course of more than fifty gatherings, a diverse range of people came to sit at the feet of Jesus: busy mothers, nurses, farmers, pastors, full-time Christian workers, counselors, internet specialists, architects, apprentices, missionaries on furlough, theologians, teachers, university students, and intercessors. Among them were the lonely, bereaved, and physically injured. There were Catholics, Lutherans, Baptists, Anglicans, Methodists, members of the Evangelical Free Church, Charismatics, and Pentecostals. They came for many reasons— to rest, to break away from their daily routine, to embark on a deeper walk with Jesus, to rekindle their first love for Jesus, or in obedience to His call. Some of their stories are included below:

> "I'm longing to learn how to hear God speak to me and to have my ears cleared out because many things steal my heart and mind away from Jesus."

> "It's a miracle that I'm here because I'm a very busy nurse. I'm longing to learn how to be quiet, and hear Him for myself, and rest in His deep love for me."

> "It's been a bit scary coming here because I do not know what will happen as we sit at Jesus's feet. But I wouldn't want to be anywhere else."

> "I've labored on the mission field for seventeen years. My desire is to come closer to Jesus's heart to hear Him speak to me about the work ahead."

"It's been a real battle for me to get here. I have a deep desire to learn to hear His voice. I realize I cannot speak to others in ministry without firstly hearing from Jesus myself."

"I've just retired, and the idea of coming to sit at Jesus's feet for a while appealed to me, particularly as I am going through a time of transition. I want to put into practice what I have learned from Him at this time."

"My work situation is very difficult. I rise at five in the morning. I don't even have time to meet with God or pray, although I love Him very much. I know I need a real change in my spiritual life, so I've come to enter into all that Jesus has for me at this time."

"I recognize that I need to lay down my whole ministry and ask, 'What do you require of me firstly, Lord Jesus, to allow you to build your church in my situation?"

"I need a richer intercessory life in order to lead my church into closer intimacy with Jesus."

"I've lost my joy because of my tiredness through constant ministry. I desire a new and deeper revelation of Jesus as my Lord—a new fire in my heart."

"There is so much emptiness amongst students, so I have come to learn how to trust Jesus for my future and know Him more intimately."

"Our church has only had a few converts after fifteen years of ministry. I'm here now to wait on Jesus and to know the way forward under His hand."

"The need of the people in Moldova is overwhelming. After seven years of ministry, I'm back at home, recuperating from health problems. Friends encouraged me to come and join others to sit at the feet of Jesus."

"My ministry is intercession. I love to join others who desire to sit at the feet of Jesus simply just to be. I want to hear the rhythm of God's heart for the city in which I live."

A teenage girl who had recently finished college attended because she had dedicated the first six months of her adult life to the Lord and could think of no better way of crowning this time than by sitting at His feet. Without exception, the common need of those who came was "their hunger and thirst" to draw closer to Jesus.

Clarity and Perspective

The participants' need for a deeper relationship with Jesus indicates that something essential is missing in the foundations of our Christian life. Many confessed they were not being fed spiritually at their home church and had allowed busy-ness and affluence to compromise their loyalty to Jesus. Could it be that we no longer understand the way Jesus intends us to live as His disciples—in simplicity and with a clear view of His priorities?

Have we lost sight of the wood for the trees—the religious structures that surround us?

Wherever we gathered to meet with Jesus, it would usually take at least a day or two for people to let go of their busy-ness and lay down their burdens (finances, family, work, and church) and come to a place where they were able to hear what Jesus wanted to say to them. As we began to hear His voice, we also felt His tender love and received His assurance that He was waiting to share the secrets of His heart with us.

Early in one meeting, the Holy Spirit dropped Psalm 131 into our hearts, reminding us that we were like weaned children, totally under Jesus's care. This led the group to thank Him spontaneously for the privilege of coming to sit at His feet—a sweet beginning to the week.

Struggles and Breakthroughs

On some occasions, we encountered difficulties. One participant persisted in presenting her own strong views about how to sit at Jesus's feet, which bore little resemblance to the way the Holy Spirit was leading the meetings. After her continued insistence, the group graciously gave her the floor while they stayed tuned to the Holy Spirit. We later received a letter asking us for her forgiveness. Jesus is so gracious in His quiet guidance.

Another person was unable to accept the Word of God at face value; she needed a logical explanation for everything. Her family debated and analyzed issues at the dinner table every night. Intellectual reasoning was of prime importance to her.

She eventually recognized her difficulties in accepting God's Word unconditionally but did not show any noticeable change of heart, even though we prayed with her until the early hours of the morning. When she returned to sit at Jesus's feet three years later, to our joy, we found a new woman—one who was deeply at peace with Jesus and herself and very sensitive to receiving His Word. We underestimate Jesus's faithfulness to impart His words of life in difficult circumstances.

On another occasion, there was a battle to freely worship Jesus. People seemed to be unsettled. The Enemy tried to bring discontent and confusion among the group. This revealed that many wanted a time of personal ministry, even though they knew that they had primarily come to sit at Jesus's feet. They had great difficulty being still to simply wait on Jesus. The group was obviously under spiritual attack. The worship leader pressed on quietly, leading us in songs of worship, which, in time, opened up a way for Jesus to express His care and love for each one. Jesus had come to heal their wounds, inviting them to touch the hem of His garment.

As we continued to worship Jesus, a brother named Hans, who noticed that one of the leaders was having trouble with his feet, asked if he could pray for him. However, the leaders discerned that Jesus wanted them to wash everyone's feet. This wonderful time of ministry, prompted by Jesus, dissipated the earlier confusion. Oh, Your ways are indeed marvelous, Lord Jesus, far beyond our understanding. The group then received a strong word of exhortation:

> "Look at My Word. Look at it with open eyes and open
> hearts. Look at it and eat it. You have come to sit at

My feet, and if you want to draw near to Me, then you must eat My Word. Why have you eaten My Word as if it was just popcorn? It is the richest of food. It gives you life. Oh, My loved ones, eat My Word. Eat and eat as you have never eaten before. Take Me seriously—eat My Word and it will change you into My likeness. Eat and eat, and you will hear Me speak to you as you have never heard Me speak before. My words are life and love. It is at your doorstep. Come and feed on My Word" (Schloss Craheim, Germany).

All week, we had been admiring a bowl of thirty choice roses on a table in the meeting room, assuming that they were part of the decorations. The true purpose of the roses was revealed as we shared Communion. While the leaders moved around the room, praying for each person, the Holy Spirit prompted Hans to follow after them to give each person a rose—a love token from Jesus. Later, we discovered that one of the ladies in the group had brought the roses, believing that Jesus had a special purpose for them. Each rose was blood red.

Spirit to Spirit

There is a world of difference between knowing God's Word and living in its power. How we need both His Spirit as well as His Word, alive and vibrant in us. As we build a strong "spirit to Spirit" relationship with Jesus, we come into the place where His Word naturally becomes our daily "bread," the place where the Holy Spirit anoints all our thoughts, where our lives reflect Jesus's heart and character, and where the ministry and gifts of the Holy Spirit flow freely. Do you remember the final word during the Canberra gathering? "It is the Spirit who gives life; the flesh profits nothing. The words that I speak to you are spirit, and they are life" (John 6:63).

Capturing Our Attention

The Gospels illustrate the way that Jesus sometimes spoke a penetrating word to capture the attention of people. Early in several of our gatherings, there was often an emphasis on specific things. Here is one such word, received in Türmberg, Germany, that touched the group deeply:

> "You want to make Me Lord, but you do not know where to begin. Relax because it is different for every one of you. My ways are personal. I speak to each one individually. Just rest in Me and trust Me to share My heart with you at the right moment. How I rejoice that you want to be with Me. It gladdens My heart as you sit in My presence. Just taste and see that I am good. Yes, again I say just taste and see that I am good for your whole person: spirit, soul, and body. My bride, it is now time to prepare yourself for the testing days that are coming for the church, and I want to teach each one of you to hear My voice personally. There is no other way to hear My voice than through My Word and My Spirit. This will prepare you for the time when they take My Word from you. You must learn to hear My Spirit speaking in many ways. Do you know how important it is for you to be here today? Treasure it. You are sowing seeds for eternity. I want you to be My voice to a world that is blind and

lost, who are searching and do not know where to find Me."

As people responded to this word about Jesus speaking to us individually, He showed us our critical spirits and reminded us of the scriptures about not judging one another (Matthew 7:1–5; Romans 2:1–16) and loving one another (John 13:34-35). We needed to relate more deeply to each other "spirit to spirit," not just in the natural human way. In His eyes, we are precious jewels, and we need to see each other that way as well. This is costly—it hurts our old selves. It is the battle between the flesh and the spirit as seen in Romans 8:1–17, leading us to the place of brokenness.

In Franklin, North Carolina, this first word challenged the group:

> "I come and walk among you today, and I bring the bounty of My grace. I am here to change you into My likeness. Is that your desire? Then listen, for I have much to say. For some it will be easy. For others, it will not be easy, but I do all things well. One word from My mouth will change you. Are you ready? Will you let Me change you? Then open your hearts. I will take each one of you by the hand and lead you. Follow Me with all of your heart, and you will see the world around you in a new way. You will be changed by My glory. I love you, My people."

A team leader then shared about the "grace of limitations," the need to accept who we really are and be content to be members of the body of Christ to which Jesus has called us. We are not to think more highly of ourselves but to think soberly, as God has

given each one of us a measure of faith (Romans 12:3). We should resist taking on tasks too profound for us but learn to walk in the true calling of God on our lives, which brings a reward of eternal value (2 Corinthians 10:12–14).

At Ashburnham Place, United Kingdom, we were reminded:

> "I have brought you aside to test you and to train you to hear My voice. You do not see many miracles in your midst because you do not hear clearly when I speak. So often, you jump ahead of Me, and what I have prepared for you is literally nipped in the bud. Do you not see how easy it is to miss the mark? That was the greatest temptation when I walked the earth—that I should not clearly speak and carry out the words of My Father. Come, let Me encourage you. Each one of you is very precious in My sight. I will teach each one of you personally, intimately, if you have ears to hear what I say to you. It is not difficult—relax in My presence, and I will fold My arms around you, and in the strength of My comfort, you will be set free."

The response by one delegate hearing this word was to cry out about the countless times he had not been available to the Lord, having missed the mark again.

In Heiligenstadt, Germany, our days began together with this directive:

> "I have no big program for you. I rejoice that you come to be with Me. How shall My people minister

to a world crying out unless they draw close to Me? Come and lie on My breast and listen to My heart, My son, My daughter. I want to bring you to the end of all that is superficial, so much activity which is not of Me. Learn to wait until I speak."

Someone saw a picture of a field with the early morning sun sparkling on the dew-covered grass, until each drop gently flowed together to water the land. This spoke of our oneness in His church, with the blessing of God described in Psalm 133.

At the peaceful prayer center located above Amden in Switzerland, we were exhorted:

"I walk among you today to bring you to My side. I have many things on My heart that I want to share with you. Are you ready? Put aside all your burdens, and responsibilities, and your many cares. This was Mary's secret. She was able to do this and give Me her full attention. Are you willing to walk the way Mary walked? I will teach you, but you need to lay aside every weight. Then you can hear My voice. Is that too much for you? Is it? I trust it is not so, for My heart overflows with love for you. There are many things I want to share with you. Come, My people, come. I am here to love and care for you and to change you into My likeness. Come to Me. Come."

On another occasion, we were encouraged as a group while on the island of Åland, Finland:

"Some of you have had a really tough time this spring. I will heal you—permit Me to do it. Do not concentrate on what has been. I'll answer your expectations, and I'll give you more than you ever expected. So leave all your wounds and hopes at My feet so that they will not limit what I want you to receive. I will show you heaven. You will experience the kind of joy, love, humility, and courage that is in heaven in a totally new way. Serve each other in all the ways to which I urge you. I will show you new and surprising ways of serving each other, and you will all have something to add."

"You are My body—I am your head. No one else is—none of the leaders. I am the head of My body, and I need all of you. I want all of you to participate. I want you to show each other My kingdom, so do not say that you are too young, too old, too wounded, too sinful, or anything else because you are not. You are My disciples, and I love you. I have created you, and in My eyes, you are fulfilled. I will open your eyes for each other in a new, loving way so that you can see My creation in each other and love each other. You are My disciples, and you have come here because I called you. What I am going to pour over you is going to echo in the whole of Finland and then the Nordic countries, and it will meet another echo in Europe. I'll speak to all of you individually and as a group, in the mornings, in the evenings, and in the afternoons; I'll speak to you and be with you all the time. Thank you for obeying My call. Thank you for being My disciples. Thank you for being here. I love you."

The next morning, one of the leaders shared, "I woke up with a sweet agony of Jesus's love for His church. It was an unusually sweet spirit but also with the touch of His pain for the indifference of many towards His strong bridegroom love for us all." This was followed by a further word from Jesus: "I have mercy on you, even though I know everything about you. Yes, I love you with an everlasting love. I have only one question for you. Do you love Me?"

Near a sunny beach at Caloundra, Australia, the group was challenged at the outset of the meeting:

> "All mankind is gathering together, seeking for a Messiah—searching, groping, longing, wondering—and yet they do not see Me. Even My church does not understand. She is so busy. Her heart is set on pleasing Me, yet she does not know Me. Will My people find Me for who I am? I want to reveal Myself in all My fullness. Can't you see that time spent with Me, doing nothing, is the beginning of true faithfulness? I love you for the work you do, but I love you more for who you are. How I long for a people who will be still and seek Me. Set your hearts aside from all I have given you to do. Learn to take time aside with Me, and we will commune together, Spirit to spirit. I

 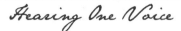

will share My heart more intimately with you. How else is the world going to find Me unless you find Me first, knowing even My smallest desire and My every wish to redeem My body into the fullness of her bridal role? That is the measure of intimacy I desire with you. How I desire to impart this to My body throughout the earth. Come and spend time with Me, and we will change many things together."

The Lord is knocking at the door of our hearts. Can you hear Him? (Revelation 3:20). Do not hesitate or be fearful. As soon as we open the door, He is ready to "dine with us" to draw us closer in sweet fellowship. Be bold. Open the door of your heart to Him now.

On one occasion before leaving home, Jesus prepared us for the unexpected with practical words:

"Be at peace as you go. I have all things in hand. Be watchful, as you travel, for the sneaky things that our Enemy will attempt to do, but also remember that I have defeated him. Be on your spiritual toes and yet be at rest. I am sending you among the hungry, the lost, and the bruised to pour out upon them the ointment of My love to heal their wounds and to calm their souls. It is better that you do a little than too much, as your bodies are now frail. Again I say take one day, one moment at a time, and I will guide you and do the rest. I have some surprises for you to share with others. Be generous to the extreme and have no fears, for I am with you."

This word had its application in Amden, Switzerland, where some of the bruised and wounded whom Jesus told us to expect had gathered. There were people on crutches, a lady recovering from a brain tumor operation with her arm in a sling, a man with only one lung who had to sit near the window to get fresh air, a woman with her ankle bound up, a young man with depression, and a full-time Christian worker suffering from burnout. During the days together, Jesus's healing balm and the ointment of His love were quietly evident among these needy ones. Jesus encouraged them:

> "I have come amongst you to heal you. You all need healing in different ways. I have come to stand amongst you as you gather together. Take time each day to thank Me for your deliverance from the ravages of this world, and I will do wonders amongst you. Do not forget to do this. It is a simple request of Mine, but it is very important. Do not delay in this matter, be diligent. Step by step, I will bring healing into the souls of each one of you. Stay close to Me. I am longing to share My heart with you. I love you all deeply."

There were times when Jesus encouraged the ministry team directly to edify individuals and the group as a whole. While on the island of Åland, Finland, He reassured one of the leaders:

> "Silently, silently I work in the hearts of My people. You need not be concerned at what I am doing among them. They are Mine, blood-bought. I cherish them day by day as they grow in My grace and pleasure.

Store up for yourself righteousness. You have sown, and in time, there will be a reaping. Fear not, for I am with you."

Exposing Fear and Anxiety

During the worship at the beginning of a meeting with a group in Germany, one of the team posed a question from Jesus; "Ask the people why they come here to worry?" He wondered if this was really the Lord speaking. He reasoned that this was unlikely to be their motive for coming to spend time with Jesus. Nevertheless, in obedience, the leader shared this word with the group. Immediately, an elderly lady exclaimed, "How do you pray for your children without worrying?" This revealed the hidden fears constantly binding some people. In a remarkable way, through the Word of God and the testimony of others who had faced similar situations, Jesus's initial prompting spontaneously established an openness and transparency in the group—something that continued throughout their days together.

At the start of a morning meeting in Switzerland, Jesus prompted one of the team to suggest that each person should go aside and spend time to discover more about Him through His Word and then share his or her discovery with the group. A young woman serving her apprenticeship as a baker excused herself from reporting back as she felt too shy to speak publicly. We anticipated that the other twenty people in the group would have enough time to share their discoveries that evening. This was not to be. It took another four sessions for everyone to describe how Jesus had revealed Himself in many new ways. The kaleidoscope of their discoveries was amazing.

We were about to close the meeting when Barbara encouraged the apprentice baker to share, despite her initial reticence. She exploded with her discoveries about Jesus, showing us a colored sketch she had drawn, conveying something of her understanding of the glory of the Lord. It was not unlike the wheels with the cherubim portrayed in Ezekiel 10:9. Was this the same shy person? Clearly, she had met the living Word Himself.

During one meeting in Åland, Jesus guided a team leader to ask each person to introduce themselves to someone they did not know and to spend quality time together during the week. One of the team was led by Jesus to an elderly man who had come to the gathering for the first time with his wife. As the leader approached him, he surprisingly cried out, "I am afraid!" It transpired that he had an important role in interpreting government legislation, where he could work by himself. This job suited him because he was fearful of mixing with other people. He shared that as a child, he had to flee with his parents from enemy troops invading their nation. Sadly, his parents could not agree where to live during the crisis, which eventually led to their separation. His mother took him further away from the conflict zone, permanently breaking his relationship with his father. This laid the foundation for deep insecurity in his life. By the end of the week, through the Holy Spirit's guidance and the promises of God's Word, he was wonderfully released from fear into Christ's freedom through the gentle caring ministry of others.

Where Are the Pastors and Leaders?

While at Amden in Switzerland one year, Jesus encouraged a group of German pastors with a specific word:

> "I am with you to guide you and lead you if you will listen to My voice, and if you do not take notice of man. It is extraordinary in My sight that My busy servants are willing to come aside to be with Me. I shall not disappoint you. It shall be according to My purpose, and not according to your understanding. Be sensitive to My Spirit. Do not be hasty to fill in the gaps. Just be, in Me, and find your true rest in Me. There may be confusion amongst you for a time. Do not be concerned. I am doing things My way. All of you will be richer for the time you have given Me to speak to you. Fear not, I am with you."

Although these pastors had resolved to come aside to be with Jesus, they were battling to let go of their responsibilities, which ranged from worldwide evangelism, to teaching God's Word, to ministering to the poor and to children. For years, we had been asking the Lord for an opportunity to bring pastors aside to sit at His feet. It was noticeable how quickly they recognized their shortcomings as they lay prostrate confessing their sins openly to Jesus, giving the Holy Spirit far greater liberty to speak to them in their leadership roles.

One Foundation

In Sydney, Australia, Jesus shared the following words at an Asia–Pacific gathering of medical and health-care professionals:

> "As you have set time aside to meet with Me, I will come and walk amongst you. I see that your hearts are open to receive My living words. Do not fear, I have come to encourage you, to strengthen you, and to lead you on. There is much work to be done for My kingdom because the days are short. Fear not, I will lead those who have open hearts and open ears to follow Me. I will lead you through the confusion of this age, and you will do mighty exploits for God, exploits born of My Spirit and birthed in the power of My Word. Oh, all I ask is that you have an open heart and a listening ear to obey Me, and I will surely lead you."

The group was challenged to examine the foundations of their work for Jesus. Their insights, which could apply to any area of Christian ministry, are summarized as follows:

- Check the foundations of the work you are involved in—are they true and honorable? Was the character of God openly proclaimed and acknowledged when the spiritual cornerstone was laid?
- What were the motives and goals of the founders? Did they fully lay the foundation of the work in Jesus or did they build a monument to glorify others?

- Ask the Lord to expose any false foundations that may have been laid by others and then seek Him to lay the foundations afresh in Christ.

Essential One-ness

At a meeting of leaders of an evangelistic ministry in Africa, who had set time aside to spend a week at Jesus's feet, the Holy Spirit simply directed their attention to John 15:5, "I am the vine and you are the branches. He who abides in Me, and I in him, bears much fruit, for without Me you can do nothing."

At the individual level, Jesus told each one, "Let go of your busyness and the turmoil in your mind. I want you to listen to Me as I speak, to assure you of My love, and to bring you to a new depth of relationship with Me."

At the corporate level, Jesus enlarged the group's understanding about the importance of true teamwork.

> "I want to knit you together according to My perfect pattern. Let Me do this, and you will be part of a beautiful new garment. Each of you intertwined, joined together, interdependent, none more special than the other. Each of you is an integral and essential part of the new thing I am planning for you. So submit to Me."

Those gathered realized how much they were working as individuals and functioning in their own strength. Our failing has been to say to others, "I have no need of you." It was a time for them to mend their nets and repair their relationships so that every part of the ministry was working effectively. Jesus encouraged these leaders by saying:

> "I will come and dwell among you today. Do not be hasty. There is plenty of time to do the things I propose to do among you. Say to one another, 'This is the day that the Lord has made. Rejoice and be glad in it.' Comfort one another with words of My life. Encourage one another with My words of strength and joy. It is time to give up your own ways and to learn to follow Me—and I am with you to do it—today."

The leaders later shared what Jesus revealed to them about working as a team:

- We need to ask Jesus to lead us, one with the other, into the joy of fellowship as leaders to experience the beauty of our community.
- Our ministry needs to quickly come to the point of totally surrendering our corporate lives to the Lord.
- Each one of us needs to lay down our own preconceived ideas on the altar to clear the way for Jesus to guide us corporately.
- As a ministry, we have not realized the full range of His gifts among us. We need a greater sense of our appreciation for one another.
- It is essential that we draw on Jesus's promises of our oneness in Him (seen in John 17:20–23) to be effective in His church and His mission to the world.

- We are having spiritual surgery under Jesus's hands to prepare us for the ministries He has for us in the future.
- As we bond together, other things will fall into order, allowing Jesus to release more of His fullness for the purposes of this ministry.

Many times, the impact of Jesus's words would grow on us as we meditated on what He shared with us. The Holy Spirit would lead us forward through specific scriptures into times of prayer, proclamation, and corporate ministry. These words of Jesus, and the various responses we have shared with you, are only a taste of what He imparted to those who gathered to sit at His feet. We experienced, to a greater depth, His promise that "wherever two or three gather in My name, there am I with them" (Matthew 18:20).

4. WORSHIP OPENS THE WAY

As you have seen from our story so far, worship is instrumental in bringing us into the presence of Jesus. He does, indeed, inhabit the praises of His people (Psalm 22:3). On every occasion, we observed how worship and adoration prepared the way for the Holy Spirit to take the initiative to speak to us and draw us closer to Jesus. Andrew Murray[2] captures something of the importance of worshiping God. He wrote:

> To worship is our highest glory. We were created for
> fellowship with God; of that fellowship, worship is
> the most sublime expression. All the exercises of our
> Christian life—meditation and prayer, love and faith,
> surrender and obedience—culminate in worship.
> Recognizing who God is in His holiness, His glory and
> His love, and realizing who I am as a sinful creature,
> and as the Father's redeemed child, I gather up my
> whole being in worship and present myself to my
> God. I offer Him the adoration, and the glory, which
> is His due. The truest, fullest and nearest approach to
> God is worship. Every sentiment and every service of
> our Christian walk is included in it. To worship God is
> our highest destiny, because in it God is all.

There is a difference between praise, thanksgiving, and worship. Worship is not limited to the fresh, creative songs that are now

---

[2] A. Murray, *The Spirit of Christ* (Minnesota: Bethany House Publishers, 1979).

sung in many churches. As uplifting as these songs are, they do not bring us into the richer realms of worship. Praise and thanksgiving, birthed out of our response to a revelation of the holiness and attributes of God are a prelude to entering into worship. This cannot be explained; it can only be revealed. Worship springs from the attitude of the heart, which leads us to respond in awe and holy fear.

Our First Priority

Our prime calling is to be incense bearers—to reflect the Lord's glory through our worship and carry the fragrance of Christ through our lives. This begins in the secret place of His presence, through our personal worship and adoration of Christ day by day. In this way, we are strengthened to be salt and light in the cauldron of everyday life. Pastors and ministry leaders have a responsibility to carry Jesus's presence into the midst of their congregations. It is important that those who lead in worship and adoration are worshipers themselves. Let us remember that we are all called to enter into worship and to be ready to give or receive a word from Him when we are assembled together.

Entering into Holy-Spirit inspired worship should be our first priority as we gather together. When this happens, everything else follows in order. As we relate Spirit to spirit, it sets the stage for the Lord to minister to us at a deeper level, and God's Word becomes much more powerful and penetrating. Worshiping in this way opens our hearts to His life-giving words and to the gifts of His Spirit. The potential is enormous when worship is our highest end.

This has been emphasized by Bob Sorge[3], a well-known pastor and worship teacher, who explains the difference between the usual Sunday service song list and learning to follow the river of God in corporate worship.

Jesus's Heart Cry

This message was brought home to us during a meeting in Finland, when Jesus shared the following word with the group:

> "Now you see that I have called you to be worshipers first and then workers. Practice your priesthood of worship, for I have called you to be kings and priests to Me. As you do this, I will pour out the Spirit of praise upon you, and I will lift you up to reign with Me. I will purify you as you worship Me. When you worship, it is like a light. I see you all like lights shining brightly. You are Mine. You belong to Me. Receive My blessings. Come quickly; run. Your heart is thirsty. I want to share My Kingdom with you; come quickly. I will put this longing to be with Me in your heart, to sing songs of worship to Me; come quickly. Stand in the strength of My authority that I give to you to bring those whom I have invited into My Kingdom. You can show them the way I love you, the way I give Myself to you and share My glory with you. You are My people. I want to share Myself with you. I come to you who labor. My yoke is easy and My burden is light. In all of your

---

[3] B. Sorge, *Following the River: A Vision for Corporate Worship* (Kansas City: Oasis House, 2004).

circumstances, worship and thank Me. I am worthy of all of your worship" (Åland, Finland).

On another occasion in Switzerland, Jesus shared His heart's cry for His church.

"Why do you look around you? Look to Me. I am the God of all ages. I am the God for your time, and I am rising up from My throne. I am calling you forth as a people from the four corners of the earth. They shall come to Me because they adore and worship Me. Adoration fills their hearts. This is the people I am calling. Before anything else, I desire worshipers. Will you be a worshiper too? Will you put every weight aside and come and worship Me? For I am your God. I desire your fellowship. I say it again: I deeply desire your fellowship. It is very precious to Me" (Amden, Switzerland).

A memorable example of the power of worship in releasing His presence occurred at a meeting in Franklin, North Carolina, at the Christian Training Center International. This was originally a country inn, set in twelve acres of redwoods, which the Lord directed Jay and Sally Fesperman to buy without telling them why. Sometime later, under the ministry of Larry and Susan Pons, this property was developed as a place of healing and restoration to families and leadership training for young people. About ninety people crowded into the upstairs lounge, complete with a massive stone fireplace and mounted deer antlers. One of the local music team, sensitively gifted in leading God's

people into Jesus's presence, led the worship on his guitar. Jesus responded with an opening word:

> "Two sparrows are sold for a penny, but your lives are priceless. Do you always see it that way? That is how I see you. Even from your conception, I have measured your life. I have tested your hearts, I have wooed you with My love, and I have shaped you, and there is yet more to come. As you sit at My feet, will you not only listen to My words, but take them into your hearts? Will you let Me continue to shape and change you into My likeness? Will you give Me permission? I have given you a free will. This is an important question, and it will cost you change and renewed direction. The days are short. I am about to bring My body together as never before. I am doing this throughout the earth because your lives are priceless. I need you to be in the place I have prepared for you this very hour. Let Me take hold of the reins of your hearts and let Me prepare you and lead you. Will you give Me your permission?" (Franklin, North Carolina, United States).

Identity Redefined

In Switzerland, our host, Werner, shared his heart before leading us in worship on his guitar: "I am not a very accomplished musician, but I am a worshiper." That set the tone for the week right from the outset.

Worship is not spiritual therapy. It is the expression of our joy in beholding Jesus and His glory. As the Holy Spirit continually sings within us in adoration, our worship is like a perpetual fire burning on the altar of our hearts (Leviticus 6:13).

One of the leadership team had a potent experience of how important our worship is to the Lord. He was leaving a meeting early when Jesus said to him, "Are you going to leave just as I am coming to minister to My people?" The leader quietly returned in anticipation of what would transpire. As the meeting was coming to a close, two elderly ladies seemed unmoved by the Lord's presence, yet they were the first to come forward to joyfully accept the baptism of His Spirit. There was a tangible sense of Jesus walking among the people, gently ministering His love and care to each one:

> "I come into your midst tonight that you might possess your possessions. Why are you satisfied with such a small portion as if you are on a diet? I have come to give you all the riches of My person. I have prepared them all for you, My people, so you will rise up as an army and do mighty exploits. From this day onwards, let Me draw you nearer and woo you, so that you will grow into the fullness I have for you. This is what I have come to do amongst you" (Deggingen, Germany).

Set Free from Religious Tradition

Jesus comes to break us out of our religious mind-set and to lead us into a richer understanding of His ways and the power of His resurrection life available to us through the miracle of His redemption. For our part, we are called to carry His light every

day, with hearts bathed in worship and filled with thanksgiving. Jesus wants to be the first love of our lives and have us willingly surrender to Him those other things we hold dear:

> "It is My heart's desire that My people will come to worship Me with uncluttered hearts. I desire My church to enter into a deeper relationship with Me. Will you make a sacrifice of thanksgiving to Me? Will you give Me all of your life? I receive your dedication to Me, and I love you deeply. Why do you still hold back that one area, that one thing? Why, when I am your All in All? My children, now that you have come into My presence, will you give Me a sacrifice of thanksgiving from the very depths of your being? Then I will change you into My likeness, if this is your heart's desire" (Ashburnham Place, United Kingdom).

There is nothing unique about these illustrations—they are already occurring in the body of Christ today. We share them with you to emphasize that Jesus's creative ministry is released when we simply come to sit at His feet to worship and wait upon Him. Jesus reminds us of His joy when we worship Him:

"I rejoice as I see you worshiping Me. You are a microcosm of My people right across the earth, coming from many churches to worship Me and to seek My face. I shall speak to you, and you shall hear My voice. I am with you" (Åland, Finland).

On a number of occasions, the Holy Spirit responded to our worship for a specific purpose that Jesus desired. For example, the following word was received by a gathering of pastors, ministry leaders, their wives, and some intercessors in the hamlet of Hubmersberg, a rural community in Germany, of two farms, about ten houses, and a traditional Bavarian hotel:

> "As you bow your hearts before Me, I receive your worship. I know your heart's desire is to draw closer to Me; I desire the same thing. Come and lay down your burdens at My feet; come. Why do you hesitate? Come and lay your burdens down so that My Spirit and Word will give you the refreshment of life. You have not come together to be in meetings, but to be with Me. You are My friends, yes, friends. I want to have fellowship with you, but that depends upon the transparency of your hearts towards Me. Come, lay down your burdens. Come. Share your hearts with Me" (Hubmersberg, Germany).

Birthing Something New

During a vibrant time of worship, a team leader shared a picture he received of a delivery room in the maternity ward of a hospital, where chaos reigned among the medical team because their normal procedures were in disarray.

A midwife in the group shared her understanding of the picture based on the pain of labor during birth. She explained that, despite pain and feelings of anxiety associated with childbirth, the experience of joy and wonder of being a new parent is worth the pain involved in bringing a child into the world. The important role of the midwife, working alongside the new mother, helps to avoid unexpected complications. The delivery room speaks of us, the church. Are we ready to accept the Holy Spirit's help as He brings forth new birth, a new passion for Jesus within the church? Or are we so set in our ways that confusion and chaos are likely to occur? Our attitude will be tested because there is pain involved in changing our ways. Failing to cooperate with the Holy Spirit will only bring further complications within the church.

Psalm 139:13-17 portrays God's loving hand in nurturing the wonder of natural birth. Will we be ready to respond to the Lord's Word in verses 23-24 to bring us into a place of order and peace during a time of renewed spiritual birth in His church to allow the Holy Spirit to work freely amongst us?

Our response should be to surrender our hearts afresh to Jesus because His death and sacrifice were costly—priceless, in fact. Through His pain and shed blood, Jesus opened the way for a new, redeemed covenant community to be shaped into His likeness. He gave Himself *for* us so that He may live freely *in* us, empowering us to live in the fullness of His love.

A Deeper Love for Jesus

As we continued to worship Jesus during the gathering at Hubmersberg, we expressed our desire for a deeper relationship with Him with a cry that words and feelings could not express, to which He responded, "I have been longing and waiting for you to seek a deeper love relationship with Me. Bow and receive this gift now. Be quiet so that you can hear what I say to you. You are My bride. I take you by your hand and draw you to Myself."

This word was followed by a time of awe and silence, while the Holy Spirit graciously birthed a deeper love for Jesus in our hearts to strengthen us to live each day in the fullness of liberty described in Galatians chapter 5. Each one of us then spent time with Jesus, placing our fears and failures before Him, expecting to receive the full dimensions of this word.

The time with Jesus at Hubmersberg breathed His life afresh into the hearts of each person. It strengthened their love for Him, healed their wounds, delivered them from their fears, and molded everyone together. The session finished in resounding worship, made still sweeter by open confession. Jesus then encouraged the group: "Rise up, My people. Come into your inheritance. Boldly give Me your heart's desire, and I shall fulfil it. Do not hold back. Ask in boldness. I have given you an open door in heaven this day."

Heavenly Dimensions, Fruitful Branches

After we worshiped the Lord at the Bartimaeus Prayerhouse, above Amden in Switzerland, which is located among local farms with majestic views across Walensee Lake to the snow-covered mountains beyond, we were encouraged:

> "I have come to be with you. I am stretching out My hand to touch your life. I breathe My Spirit upon you. Receive Me as your Lord and Savior. How I love you. You are beautiful in My sight. I made you, yes, I made you beautiful, and I have much joy in you. Open your hearts to Me, and I will share My heart with you, for this is a time of intimacy between you

and Me. Open your hearts wide. There are so many things I want to share with you this week. I cannot share them unless your heart is open. Come, let us walk and talk together. Let us share our hearts, and I will change you into My likeness. Is that your heart's desire? I am ready for sweet fellowship with you. Open your heart, and I will fill it with a new depth of My love."

Jesus then spoke to us through His Word in Hebrews 12:22–24, challenging the group to take up heavenly dimensions in prayer—dimensions set so clearly above our earthly limitations. This was followed by a song in the Spirit, a song of hope to the bride:

"I call you from the desert places. I call you from the four corners of the earth. Come quickly. Come, follow Me to green pastures and to still waters. There I will show you My love. Come from all of your busy-ness. Come, and I will show you more of Myself and share My heart and My love with you. Oh, My bride, My beautiful one, how else can I share My heart unless you come quickly to share your heart with Me?"

To this, in the flow of further worship, the Lord added, "I'm coming soon, and I desire you to be a fruitful branch for My kingdom."

John 15:1–5 reveals three prerequisites for being a fruitful branch. First, we need to be grafted into the vine through our new birth in Christ. Second, we must depend upon Him in all circumstances and have undoubting confidence in His guidance. Third, we must continue abiding in Him. *The Message* translation says it beautifully: "I am the Vine and you are the branches. When you're joined with Me, and I with you ... the harvest is sure to be abundant."

A tall, espaliered pear tree growing up a gabled stone wall of a two-storied house in Switzerland provided a vivid picture of fruitfulness. Its horizontally extended branches were laden with beautiful, ripe pears, even though it was planted among stone paving. This pear tree showed us that our lives should bear abundant fruit for Jesus, regardless of our circumstances.

Let us grasp the reality that we can do nothing of any eternal value unless we receive it from heaven (John 3:27). That is why it is so essential to come and sit at Jesus's feet. Grace is the origin of everything we receive: yes, grace leading to faith. The issue is to bear fruit in our lives, yet many of us are focused on producing results through our works for God. We can only bring our fruit into heaven, not our well-meaning good works. Bearing fruit is the outcome of an intimate relationship with Jesus, and this can only be born of His Spirit.

Angel's Food

Tampere is the third largest city in Finland, set among a group of lakes and surrounded by forests of spruce, birch, and pine. The local church community was in a state of flux as the leaders grappled with the changes taking place in their fellowship. They wanted to know God's will and future direction for the church.

Following a time of worship at the beginning of the first meeting, Jesus provided this word to guide them:

"Come, leave your burdens and duties behind. Give Me your full attention and be sensitive to the Holy Spirit. He will touch your heart, and I will sing over you to bring you closer and closer to Me. I embrace you with My love. Receive My love; it is strong and rich, prepared for you, My bride."

Through true worship, Jesus can inspire a prayer, a song, or a verse of scripture for us to sing or speak prophetically over a situation, even over a nation. Worship releases His powerful purposes in the spiritual realm:

> "It gives Me great joy when you rise up and worship Me. This is angel's food because praises and worship minister to My heart. Come, My daughters, My sons, sing the songs of the Lord. This is why I give you voices—to sing My songs over the nations, over your land, over your villages and homes. As you sing, I send out angelic hosts. You are My instruments to sing My songs. Come, sing My songs."

The Lord followed with a Word from Haggai 1:6–11, warning us about barrenness. As the group sat in silence in Jesus's presence, meditating on this Word, one of the elders shared a picture of a pan flute with only one pipe functioning, and with it came the word "finance." The broken pipes represented the missing ministry gifts among the various elders and the fact that money had become their focus. For the flute to sound sweet again, these pipes—personal relationships among the elders—would have to be repaired. Readings from 2 Corinthians 5:16–17 and Hebrews 10:22–25 were followed by prayer, which resulted in all the elders being bonded together in a godly order. Each elder was also released into their callings and gifts. Jesus then imparted a word of counsel to them:

> "Start walking and talking with Me, and I will bring you into My freedom. This is what I have come to do amongst you today. It will be different for each one of you. Do not continue to judge one another by your standards. This is My responsibility. Be assured of My love and mercy. Come and ask Me what it means to walk and talk with Me. I will bring light and understanding into your hearts, and you will begin to see with My eyes, hear with My ears, understand with My mind, and love with My heart. If you obey My Word to you, you will be changed into My likeness. Nothing is more sure."

Unusual Obedience

At this point, Noel remembered a word he had received some time earlier from an intercessor friend, challenging him to be ready, at the Holy Spirit's prompting, to dance before the Lord. Here in Tampere, the moment came for him to obey.

It took some courage to start dancing at the age of seventy-eight while singing a gentle song in the Spirit! Later, Noel was asked why he got up and danced. As Noel explained his need for obedience, he sensed that those present were also learning to follow the prompting of the Holy Spirit and were being freed from the fear of others' opinions. Oh, how we need to leave everything in Jesus's hands, confident that the Holy Spirit will guide us.

Dancing was also featured at the gathering in Franklin, United States. Worship burst out spontaneously one morning with song and dance as we opened up our hearts to Jesus. The Lord then encouraged the group:

> "In times like these, when My people gather together, there is a heavenly host surrounding you with a crescendo of praise. Now that I have your attention, I pour out My love upon you, and I come to teach you My ways so that My glory shall be manifested on the earth. Come and sit at My feet at this time and listen, and I will speak. Love one another and be filled with My joy, and I will change others through My love in you. Do not miss any opportunity to love one another."

These stories are illustrations of service for the Kingdom of God that is offered to Jesus in wholehearted worship that flows from every fiber of our being. We need to offer all the fruitfulness that Jesus has brought forth through our lives back to Him as an act of our fervent love and worship. The Puritan, John Piper, recognized this long ago when he wrote, "The chief end of man is to glorify God by enjoying Him forever."

5. SITTING IN SILENCE

After the many times of worship and adoration as we sat at Jesus's feet, we often found ourselves waiting in silence and awe of Jesus's presence among us. The silence stilled our hearts and minds, bringing us to a place where we were content to wait until Jesus took the initiative.

Silence is important because when our words are few, we can hear Jesus speak more clearly. Ecclesiastes 5:2 sums up the significance of silence clearly: "Do not be rash with your mouth and let not your heart utter anything hastily before God. For God is in heaven and you on earth. Therefore let your words be few." How important it is for us to come to a place of quiet rest through the discipline of solitude and silence. We are exhorted to "be still and know that I am God" (Psalm 46:10-11).

To be still, we must not only stop speaking, but learn to silence our own thoughts and feelings as well. It takes the Holy Spirit's cleansing "whoosh" within us to really let go of everything else and be ready to listen to Jesus in silence. Our reward will be "the submissive wonder of reverence which bursts forth in praise" (Psalm 65:1 Amplified).

After sitting in silence with Jesus, you become aware of His fragrance resting upon you, gently possessing your whole being (2 Corinthians 2:14-16). Your perspective on everyday life is purified, and the dross of the world loses its influence on you.

A Constant Battle

It is so easy for us to follow our own thoughts instead of being still as we wait before Jesus. Our flesh and the Devil will do whatever they can to sidetrack us. Be watchful of things—even good things—that are always ready to capture our attention and keep us occupied so that we do not hear the gentle whisper of the Holy Spirit. The self is always ready to assert and intrude. However, our persistence in learning to die to self and to hear the voice of Jesus will be rewarded (John 10:27).

A Fast from Words

To help us learn the discipline of silence, Jesus sometimes instructed us to fast from words. On one occasion, we committed ourselves to complete silence from the end of an evening meeting until after breakfast the next day. This allowed each one of us to focus solely on Him. Fasting in this way goes against the modern way of life because unless we are busy, we do not feel that we are achieving anything. People were hesitant to do this fast at first, but later shared amazing testimonies of the rich experience they had with Jesus during this time of silence:

> "I found peace and security in God. He makes my big problems look small. He brings hidden things out into the light."

> "I learned that in silence and quietness, God reveals His will to us and changes our hearts."

"I experienced the Lord walking by my side in silent fellowship."

During a session of worship in Finland, the Holy Spirit brought the group to sit silently in Jesus's presence until He shared His heart. Jesus then helped us to understand the importance of waiting silently before Him:

> "When I was young, My Father taught Me the secret of coming aside to be in His presence, just as you are in My presence now. There were many times that words were not spoken. I knew what He was telling Me. We are one in Spirit, and I am calling you to be one in Spirit with Me. This takes time. It takes peace on your part and on My part—patience for you to let go of the world, and patience for Me to wait to be able to speak to you. Do you not see how I long to fellowship with you, Spirit to spirit, without words being spoken? Come aside and learn to be with Me in quietness. I will teach you as I begin to share My heart with you. Yes, even the secrets of My heart because we have begun to build a oneness of Spirit, so that a stronger trust is established between us."

The Language of Silence

On another occasion, the blessing of being silent in His presence was the emphasis:

> "Are you willing to change your lifestyle so that we can fellowship together in the sweetness of

silence? My still, small voice is more powerful than all the thunder and earthquakes. I long to give you My words of life in a deeper way. I am waiting for you to draw near to Me, and I will draw near to you. Even if I do not speak, is not My fellowship sufficient for you? My beloved, come follow Me into the heavenly realms I have prepared for you" (Åland, Finland).

As we wait patiently for Jesus, He has the freedom to share the depths of His heart with us. It is through the stillness of our hearts that the life of faith strikes a deeper root within us, and the Holy Spirit accomplishes the Lord's work in our lives. As the Word says, "Truly my soul silently waits for God; from Him comes my salvation" (Psalm 62:1).

When we wait silently before Him, our minds gather a wealth of knowledge and fresh revelation from His Word. In turn, this feeds our desire to fulfill His will. Our prayers take on a Holy Spirit-inspired dimension beyond the place of our natural understanding. We need to consistently put this discipline into practice.

In Franklin, North Carolina, Jesus had a special word for us about waiting in silence:

> "I did not pour out My Spirit upon you for nothing. It takes time to change you into My likeness. I cannot do it all at once because you would burst with My glory. I move gently and tenderly in your life to change you to be like Me; that's why these times

are very precious to Me. Yes, right now you are doing nothing and saying nothing. Do you know what that says to Me? You have a heart to listen, to receive, and to take in My very essence. To each one of you, this is different; it is true that I am making all things new. You will go away changed. It is important that the change continues to work through you in your home and in your workplace. Look upon this time as laying stronger foundations in Me. Gather all you can of the things I say to you here and take them into your hearts. I am laying a deeper foundation for you that will carry you through in the days to come."

At another time in Franklin, North Carolina, Jesus gave the group a taste of the blessings that can flow when silence ushers us into the secret place:

"Tonight, the alabaster box has been cracked, and it will be broken open. Tonight, My fragrance can escape and flow one drop at a time. It shall flow more and more from this day on. Do not try to repair the box. You will fail. The day will come when My beauty, loveliness, and character will flow out of you so naturally because My grace is sufficient for you. Yes, My grace abounds towards you. It overflows you. You know those failures that you have struggled to hand over to Me. How many times have we been over them together? Countless times, I have waited to break open your alabaster box. Now tonight, it is done."

During a meeting in Schloss Craheim in Germany, Jesus shared a reassuring word about His desire to be with us in quietness:

> "I want to thank you for coming to spend time with Me. You really do not know how much joy it brings to Me. How I long for My people to do this more often— simply to come and be with Me! Be encouraged; I will speak many things to you at this time. They will be simple things, pure things—My words of life. So all I ask is your total devotion to Me; and I will share My heart with you. I want to be in quietness with you; I want to hold you in My arms at this time."

By sitting at His feet, quietness and stillness naturally become part of our hidden life in Jesus, even when we are busy. We come to the place of remaining in our Father's rest. During one session, Werner Woiwode, who heads up a prayer ministry in Switzerland with his wife, Regula, led us in a simple song, "Jesus, You are Lord," over and over again, and then he fell silent, leaning on his guitar. The whole group was quietly growing more conscious of Jesus's presence, wondering what He was doing among us. Nothing seemed to be happening. Someone then began to sing "Majesty," but Werner did not take it up on his guitar. Why? Eventually, we realized that Jesus remained silent until we were ready to simply listen.

We remember some other times of precious silence while sitting at the feet of Jesus. One was when we took communion together in the middle of a meeting. The Holy Spirit created a strong desire among us to break bread and receive the cup so that we could obtain a deeper understanding of Christ's broken body

and His shed blood. The extended period of stillness with Jesus that followed was profound; we felt that we were resting on His breast. On another occasion when we waited without words, the Lord came quietly among us, almost in a tangible way.

When Jesus sees that we want to wait upon Him for His own sake, He can hardly contain Himself with joy. It really is the sweetest form of worship.

PART TWO

DEEP CALLS TO DEEP

In Part 1, "Hearing One Voice," you walked with us as we learned to sit at Jesus's feet. We trust that you are encouraged by His words of life.

In Part 2, "Deep Calls to Deep," you will discover more about how He longs for a deeper relationship with His bride so that we can know His heartbeat more intimately and He can prepare us for the days ahead.

The words presented here were given to the gathered body of Christ in several different countries over a number of years. Not surprisingly, they have a similar emphasis because the Holy Spirit was revealing many of the same things to those who gathered to sit at His feet. These words were usually received during profound times of corporate worship.

This selection of words is arranged into five broad categories and then under subheadings within each category to indicate the essence of what Jesus wanted to impart to us.

We have suggested some Bible verses to be read in conjunction with each of these "words." These verses can be used as entry points to search the scriptures for yourself in order to enhance your understanding of the Lord and His great love.

1. Jesus Calls Us to Himself

I Have Called You—Sit at My Feet—Fellowship and Communion—Waiting—Resting

2. Jesus Shares His Heart

My Heart—My Love—My Spirit—My Words—My Hand—My Voice

3. Jesus's Desire for Intimacy with Us

My Presence—Intimacy—My Bride—Changing You—My Likeness—My Strength—My Anointing

4. Jesus Looks for Our Response

Our Cries—Our Heart—Submit and Surrender—Dying to Self—Freedom—Walk and Follow—Sanctify Yourself—Kings and Priests—Songs in the Spirit

5. The Days Ahead

My Body—The Nations—Missions—The Battle—Your Inheritance—Hope—My Joy—My Glory

We trust these words are a great blessing to you, that they help you to build a more intimate relationship with Jesus, our Savior, Lord and friend, and help sharpen the focus of Jesus's purpose for your life.

1. JESUS CALLS US TO HIMSELF

I Have Called You

Set your heart at ease

"Call My people, call them together, for I have much to say to them. Dark days with storm clouds are gathering. The purposes of evil are now standing in an orderly manner as never before; they are bound together. Unless you hear Me speak, how will you know what to do and who to follow? I will show you when and where, and with whom, to meet. It is time to gather My church together so that they can learn to know what I want to say to them. So be at ease and take every word, even the familiar, deeply into your heart"

(Ashburnham Place, UK, 1997).

Matthew 24:7–8; John 10:1–5, 27–28

Set aside for His power and authority

"I have come among you to change your views. What seems to be weak will be strong. Small things will become big. Do not look at the gifts that others have received; look to Me and I will show you what to do with My power and authority. Seek Me. Do not compare yourself with others"

(Heiligenstadt, Germany, 1997).

Matthew 28:18; 2 Corinthians 12:9–10; Galatians 6:4–5

Sit at My Feet

Tasting My life

"I invite you to come and sit at My feet to taste My sweetness. Slowly, surely I have drawn you and will continue to draw you as you give Me first place in your life. I will remain by your side in the turmoil that the world manufactures. You will have a serenity birthed in your spirit that nothing can remove. Wherever I send you, draw your life out of Me"

(Franklin, United States, 1999).

Isaiah 55:1–3; Psalm 34:8–9, 105:2–5; Song of Songs 2:3

The rhythm of My heart

"Your worship gladdens My heart. I embrace it as a sweet fragrance. You are like a lovely, innocent bride to Me, but your heart is not in rhythm with Mine. Come, I am here to embrace you with My love. Why do you worry so much about the things around you? In Me, liberty is your inheritance. My bride, come and be with Me, and I will teach you how to love with a love that is born of My Father. It is your inheritance"

(Enzen, Germany, 2003).

John 15:9–17; Galatians 5:1

Fellowship and Communion

Come to Me again

"I have invited you to come and spend time with Me. I have spoken to you many times over the years. I say to you again— come, spend time with Me. In the past, you have asked Me to draw you nearer, and I have spoken words of encouragement and direction to you, but you have not continued to come to Me. You have become busy with other things. You have treated Me in a casual way and assumed that you could return at a time that is convenient to you. You have not come back to spend time with Me so that I could work in your life and cultivate the seeds that I have planted in you so that you may be fruitful. You have allowed the words that I have spoken to you to lie fallow in your spirits. Do not be foolish. I want to hear your concerns and also tell you those on My heart. Do not let the field of your life stay fallow. Allow Me to complete the work that I have begun in you. Come and seek Me on My terms while I may be found"

(Franklin, United States, 1997).

Isaiah 55:6; Hosea 10:12; Mark 4:1-8; Philippians 1:6; Revelation 2:4

Lay your burdens down

"You have come to a real place of fellowship with Me. I have arranged it this way so that you can partake of communion together, not as a ceremony and not as a climax, but in the very midst of what I am doing. It is the most important part of the work I am doing in your hearts. Although the storm clouds are moving, be at peace. In the world, there is much trouble. Fellowship with Me is your security. Each day, receive the life I breathe into you to serve Me. Do not come to Me to have your problems solved; instead, come to a place where you can trust Me more deeply. Do not look to the things of the world for security. Trust Me. Lay down your burdens and trust Me"

(Heiligenstadt, Germany, 1997).

Psalm 91:1–2; Proverbs 3:5–6; Matthew 6:33; John 16:33

Know Me in a new way

"I am walking amongst you and rejoicing in your praises. They gladden My heart and are sweet to My Spirit. I am going to reveal Myself to you in ways that you have never known before. My people are hurrying and scurrying across the face of the earth, and they have no time to listen and hear Me speak. Draw closer, let go of your fears, and I will teach you how to dine with Me in sweet fellowship. Put your head on My breast and rest. This is not a time for battle; it is a time to know Me as you have never known Me before"

(Ashburnham Place, UK, 2001).

Revelation 3:20; Song of Songs 2:3–6

Deep Calls to Deep

The fruit of longing

"As you gather together in My presence, I will draw you to Myself. You come with many concerns on your heart. I am here to heal you and restore you. Your first love has grown cold. I will breathe on you anew by My Spirit and My Word. All you have to do is to long for My fellowship and My intimacy and the sweetness of My presence. It is as simple as that. Come, let us have communion and fellowship with one another, for I want to share My heart with you. Are you ready to listen? Then rest, and trust in Me"

(Ashburnham Place, UK, 2003).

Revelation 2:4; Revelation 3:20

Waiting

Setting your plans aside

"Lay aside every weight and sin, which so easily ensnares you, and look to Me, the author and finisher of your faith. Set your plans aside. Continue to sit and wait. I will direct you. Do not be hasty and run ahead. Spend more time to minister to Me, and I will open up the way. I will take you into a new measure of trust. I will not fail you. Will you wait?"

(Pretoria, South Africa, 1997).

Psalm 25:4–10; Hebrews 12:1–2

Letting Jesus take the initiative

"Take things quietly and wait for Me to lead you into the place where you can share your heart with others. Then share your relationship with Me. Share how you have grown just by being with Me each day and how this has molded your life over many years. This will open up the door for others to enter into a deeper love relationship with Me. I will take the initiative. Leave it all in My hands"

(Enzen, Germany, 2004).

Psalm 89:1–2, 14–18; Lamentations 3:25

Resting

Live one day at a time

"Why do you hold onto some things? I have laid down My life for you, so why do you not put all these things into My hands and trust Me for your future? Did I not say that you should live one day at a time and that worrying will not change anything? I will lead you into tomorrow. Right now, why do you not rest in My arms and feel My strength surrounding you? Let Me embrace you. Remain in My rest in every situation. This is My provision for you"

(Amden, Switzerland, 2003).

Psalm 31:14–16, 37:7 Proverbs 3:5–6; Matthew 6:25–34

No conditions, just rest

"There are no conditions attached to My love for you. There is nothing you have to do; just come and rest and learn of Me. I am gentle, meek, and lowly. Take My yoke upon you, and I will help you. You are not alone. I have all you need, and all that I am I will give to you. Just come to Me and rest"

(Strittmatt, Germany, 1999).

Matthew 11:28–30; 1 John 4:16

Enter into My rest

"My bride, as I prepare you for the great celebration of the marriage supper of the Lamb, I am with you in the secret place of the heart. Rest assured that you will come through this preparation with joy. As I bless and cleanse you, you will see My glory, and you will display My glory. Be content, My darling one. Rest in My love"

(Canberra, Australia, 1992).

Psalm 16:9, 11; Revelation 19:6–9

2. JESUS SHARES HIS HEART

My Heart

I long to give from My treasure

"I have gathered you here to reveal My heart and the treasure I have for you so that we can work together in a new way. Is this really what you want? Will you keep My treasure precious or use it for your own ends to gain something in this world? Examine your motives so that I can give you all that I have in My heart. Cherish what I put into your heart. It will keep you in the days to come"

(Franklin, United States, 1999).

2 Corinthians 4:7; Colossians 2:2–3

I long to share My heartbeat

"My sons and My daughters, it gives Me much joy that you have come aside to worship Me. Your worship gives Me the opportunity to share My heart with you and My will for you. I am looking for servants who will know My heartbeat, and move in obedience, and love to minister to a dying and broken world. Will you be such servants?"

(Amden, Switzerland, 2005).

Matthew 25:21; John 17:13; Ephesians 2:10, 3:17–19

His healing gaze—just be with Me

"Let Me lift the veil from your face. Let Me look into your eyes and the deep recesses of your soul. Allow Me to see you. Allow Me to know you. Allow Me to heal those things in you that would resist My gaze. Allow Me to hold you. My beloved, I understand your different situations and needs, and I am able to satisfy you, to meet you right where you are. You do not have to compare yourself to anyone else. All you have to do is be with Me. Each of you is an individual jewel making up My crown. Just be with Me where you are as I am with you. Relax in that knowledge. How I love you"

(Canberra, Australia, 1992).

Song of Songs 4:1–2; Corinthians 3:16–18

My Love

My love is steeped in sacrifice

"I have gathered you together as My sons and daughters; I have gathered you together as My friends. I desire to share so much of My heart with you. I have not come to overwhelm you; I have come to strengthen you. Please take what you have received and cherish it. Never doubt that you can accomplish the challenges I place before you if you remain in My nurturing love. The bruised and the broken, the lost and the lonely hunger for My love but do not know where to find it. Will you carry My love to them? Be assured of My love. Let Me pour it out over you and through you to touch others. My love is a sacrificial love. I want your love to be sacrificial too"

(Ashburnham Place, UK, 1997).

John 15:15; 1 John 3:1–2, 11, 16–18

My love overflows to the nations

"Your hearts are precious to Me. I am molding them into My likeness. Let all your fears go. I love you with an everlasting love. Do not waste the bounty of My love poured upon you. Let it be a river flowing out of you to the nations. How else will the nations know of My love? Receive My love and treasure it. It has been bought with My blood shed for you"

(Ashburnham Place, UK, 2000).

Ezekiel 47:1–12; Revelation 5:9–10

If only you knew

"If only you knew how precious you are. If only you could grasp the fullness of My love for you. As you receive more of My love and focus less on yourself, you will know more of My love and My kindness to you. Will you take this life of Mine—a life of mercy and love—and give it to others? Let My love abound in your heart for others. This is My desire in revealing the depths of My love for you"

(Ashburnham Place, UK, 2002).

2 Corinthians 9:8; John 3:30

My Spirit

Poured out

"I have watched you seeking to find Me, and you have been struggling. There is no need for that. My Spirit has been poured on you to anoint you and glorify Me. Be at peace. Do not let your knowledge get in the way of My Spirit. Then, you can come with freedom to worship Me and hear what I desire to say to you. My words of life will change you. I want to partner with you, and I want to send you to the four corners of the earth, but you cannot go in your own strength. Will you let Me change you into My likeness?"

(Pretoria, South Africa, 1997).

Joel 2:28–29; John 15:4; 1 Corinthians 2:12

Empowering and life-giving

"Take My words into your heart. Let them be a great treasure to your soul and your spirit. Do not neglect My Word that comes to you through My Spirit. I am not asking you to deny your humanity; I am asking you to walk by My Spirit in the liberty I have given you. You have freedom to do what you want to do, to say what you want to say, to go where you want to go. I gave you this freedom so that you may know the joy of choosing to walk and live through the power of My Spirit. All things are yours, but remember—not all things are profitable. Learn of Me; keep close to Me. Do not nullify the grace I have given you by doing your own thing. Place the words I have spoken to you into the depth of your spirit as a great treasure. Value My words to know life, and truth, and as the way to know Me and enjoy Me"

(Ashburnham Place, UK, 2000).

Proverbs 2:1–6; John 6:68; 1 Corinthians 10:23; Galatians 5:16

Searching for a people to carry My fragrance

"I am breaking open the freshness of My Spirit upon you. I want to restore you to be the people I have called you to be. My kingdom is built upon your praises. My joy and hope is in those who are totally dedicated to Me. My eyes look here and there throughout the earth for such people. Will you be among them? Will you be among My chosen ones who will carry My fragrance throughout the earth?"

(Herrnhut, Germany, 2002).

2 Chronicles 16:9; 2 Corinthians 2:15

Drawing my bride to Me

"Settle your hearts before Me. I have come to transform you. Will you allow Me to touch you in a deeper and richer way than you have known before? I want to teach you to know and cherish My Spirit in an even greater way. He will lead you in a new path I have prepared for you. How can I know My bride unless My Spirit draws you to Me? You have only begun your journey. You have only had a glimpse of your inheritance; I want you to possess it fully. I want to carry you into a new realm of living, a realm of moving and having your being in Me. Do I have your permission?"

(Ashburnham Place, UK, 2003).

Isaiah 43:19, 64:3–4; Acts 17:28

My Words

It is time to listen

"Let My Word dwell in your heart by faith and possess you. Then you will be changed into My likeness. Do you see where the battle lies? Is it My Word that gives you life, strength, and purpose, or is it the words of others? Choose from where you will draw your life. You are My sheep, and as your heart turns towards Me, you will hear Me speaking, and you will be able to follow Me without hindrance, without fear, and without doubt. I am the Lord your God. I give you My life. You are blood-bought sons and daughters. I will speak clearly to you; listen to My voice"

(Turku, Finland, 1996).

John 10:27; Colossians 3:16

Deep Calls to Deep

It is time to feast

"Listen to the words I speak to you. I am feeding you with good grain. When you know the quality of My words, oceans of things dear to your heart will pour over you. Come and dine with Me. I want to be really close to you. Do not rush ahead. Let Me take the initiative. Enjoy the words I give you; although they may be few, they will be a feast"

(Pretoria, South Africa, 1997).

Revelation 3:20; Psalm 23:5

It is time to be strengthened

"As I give food to the birds of the air, so I walk amongst you and throw the seed of My Word into your hearts. My Spirit will take My Word and feed you. Eat and be satisfied. How I long for a people who know My Word. Be on your guard because many will try to take My Word from you. Read My Word, take it, and eat it"

(Deggingen, Germany, 1998).

Psalm 119:161–162; Matthew 6:26; Mark 4:3–20

My Hand

My hand is upon you

"Do you know what it means for Me to lay My hand on you? If the storms come, the foundations will stand because My hand is on you. If the fire and waters come, I will teach you to swim into quiet waters. There will be no situation where My hand will not be upon your life. Even if the devil attacks you so that you no longer know that you are still Mine, My right hand will protect you. My hand will be upon your life through everything"

(Niedenstein, Germany, 1999).

Psalm 18:36, 31:15; Isaiah 43:1–2

Take My hand

"Reach out and take My hand; I want to lead you. I have new frontiers, new challenges, and new works prepared for you, born of My Spirit. You have wearied yourself with much good work and hours of praying, and your spirit is like lead because you have done it all in your own strength. Meanwhile, I have been waiting. Reach out and take My hand. Did I say more than this when I called My disciples? It is the same for you. Reach out, take My hand, and follow Me. That is all you need to do. I will guide you. My desire for you is to be free. I saw you and waited for you to be born in this time. Other things have tried to form you, but I have shaped you to contain My character and to be one with Me"

(Ashburnham Place, UK, 2002).

Isaiah 30:18; Mark 8:34; John 5:19–20

Place everything into My hands

"Why do you hold on to some things? I have laid down My life for you, so why do you not give Me your doubts and uncertainties? Place everything into My hands and trust Me for your future. Live one day at a time. All your worrying will not change anything. Come, put all your concerns into My hands and leave them there. Gently, I will lead you into tomorrow. Right now, rest in My embrace and feel My strength surrounding you. Learn to remain in My rest in every situation. This is My provision for you"

(Amden, Switzerland, 2003).

Psalm 55:22; Matthew 6:34; Luke 12:22–26; Hebrews 4:9; 1 Peter 5:7

My Voice

Hear My voice

"It is so easy to receive from Me and then lay My words aside. Even as I received from My Father and obeyed His Word, do the same and obey. I am bringing My people to a place where they can hear My voice and restore My testimony. If this is also your heart's desire, then draw close to Me. Set aside some of your unimportant projects so that when I send you out, you will bear much fruit. My heart's cry is that you will hear My voice"

(Nuremberg, Germany, 1996).

Isaiah 55:11; John 2:5, 10:4

Relax in Me and listen

"There are not many miracles among you because you do not hear My voice clearly when I speak. So often, you jump ahead of Me, and what I had prepared for you is nipped in the bud. It is easy to miss the mark. My greatest temptation when I walked the earth was that I should not clearly hear and speak the words of My Father. If you have ears to hear what I want to say to you, I will teach each of you personally. It is not difficult. Relax in My presence, and I will fold My arms around you. In the strength of My comfort, you will be set free. You are precious in My sight"

(Ashburnham Place, UK, 1999).

John 5:19, 30; Romans 8:32

3. JESUS'S DESIRE FOR INTIMACY WITH US

My Presence

Entering the presence of the Lord

"You are always welcome in My presence. The veil is torn apart for you to come and spend time with Me. When you are at rest and peace in My presence, it pleases Me and brings Me great joy. I know that our times together are precious to you. They are more precious to Me. When we are together, I can reveal my goodness and greatness. I can show you how to handle the hard times ahead. All that I have is for you. I long for the members of My body to know how to come into My presence, to put their trust fully in Me"

(Ashburnham Place, UK, 1999).

Psalm 16:11; Matthew 27:51

Simply come

"Do not be in a hurry for answers; I will give them to you in due time. I will lead you each day. Do not be concerned about the future. I would like My people to simply be with Me and rejoice in My presence. Take your time with Me in a relaxed way and enjoy Me. Take time to get to know Me naturally. I have come to make Myself known to My people"

(Rosenheim, Germany, 2004).

Psalm 37:7; Philippians 4:4

Intimacy

Let My life flow in you

"I stand amongst you to set you free. You are trying too hard to please Me. I did not call you into the Kingdom to live like this. I called you into the Kingdom to have an intimate relationship with Me. I invite you to put down every weight you are carrying to be a good Christian. My priorities are different from the ways in which the world has taught you to live. When you are close to Me, My life will flow into you and you will naturally be able do things based on the strength of our relationship. Come, rest in Me so that I can change you into My likeness"

(Rosenheim, Germany, 2005).

Isaiah 55:8–9; John 1:12–13, 15:4–8; Galatians 3:26

My Bride

The gift of poetry was restored to a pastor's wife by the Holy Spirit, as mentioned in chapter 1.

"Have you counted the cost of being My bride?
Are you willing to pay the price?
For the dowry I ask is all you have,
all that you are, as a sacrifice.

Yes, you will have joy, indescribable love.
But they're mingled with tears and pain.
You'll suffer the loss of approval of men,
lose your reputation and maybe your name.

Are you willing, though trembling, to do what I say?
Will you step out on the water just to obey?
I'll pour you out as incense so sweet,
to a church who's My body, till it's complete.

You'll be broken and molded to be My vessel.
Will you still come to My breast to nestle?
Do you really believe I'll be with you always?
Whatever I tell you to say or to do?
I'll strengthen, and keep you, and guide you forever.
Come, taste and see that My Word is true!"

(Canberra, Australia, 1992).

Isaiah 41:10, 64:8; Matthew 16:24–25, 28:20; Luke 14:25–34; Philippians 2:17, 3:7–12

Priceless surrender

"I search the hearts of My people for those truly surrendered to Me. This is the bride I am waiting for—a bride I can confide in, to whom I can pour out My heart. Your surrender is priceless to Me; it is a jewel in My crown. I will honor your costly submission to Me. Do not strive; surrender, and I will pour out My love upon you as never before"

(Ashburnham Place, UK, 2001).

Romans 5:5, 12:1; Zechariah 9:16

Rise up in your beauty

"You are My bride; I have no other. You are beautiful beyond your imagination. But you have let problems, doubts, and accusations rob you of your beauty. I am waiting for the day that I cannot look upon you because your beauty is too much for Me. Come now—take off your working clothes. Put on the bridal gown that I have bought with My precious blood. Wear it with confidence and be secure in your beauty. You ravish My heart, and I am waiting to be alone with you, waiting for you to be free to let Me love you with My strong bridegroom love. Come and I will teach you how to be a bride"

(Canberra, Australia, 2006).

Psalm 149:4; Isaiah 61:10; Song of Songs 4:9

Changing You

Let Me do it

"I am doing new things in your hearts. I am changing you. Do not be surprised by the things that I speak to you. I am preparing you for the work I have for you in the days to come. Do not think that you are not ready or worthy. I am preparing you so that I can send you out renewed and strengthened"

(Ashburnham Place, UK, 1998).

Isaiah 43:19; Galatians 4:19; Ephesians 2:10

My Likeness

True freedom

"I have called you to discipleship. Do not try to live the perfect life just be My disciples. Trials and testings are waiting for you every day to train you to die to yourself so that My life will grow in you. How else can I refine you and change you into My likeness? Do not be discouraged when you fail. I will be there to lift you up and lead you back to the place where you will know that your life is hidden with Me in the Father. Life in Me does not involve striving; life in Me is true freedom, even during difficult times. Take the words of life that you have received from Me and embed them in your heart. They are pearls that I have placed in you"

(Ashburnham Place, UK, 2000).

2 Corinthians 3:17, 4:7–12; Colossians 3:3

I am reality

"Feed on My Word, and you will learn to live with Me in heavenly places effortlessly and naturally. Then you will be as I intended you to be—unique and irreplaceable. Your life will be a precious jewel in My hands. The way I am transforming your heart is the beginning of teaching you how to live with Me in the Spirit while being natural to those around you. Come, take My hand and walk with Me, full of My Spirit, into the destiny and purpose that I have for your life. I will finish this journey with you if you are willing to be My disciples. Let us walk through to the fulfillment of the destiny and call that I have upon your life to glorify Me and My Father. Come with Me"

(Ashburnham Place, UK, 2000).

Romans 12:2; Ephesians 2:6

Deep Calls to Deep

My Strength

Humble yourself

"Come and receive My heavenly strength. My hand is upon you. Do not step back. I never come to you in hardness of heart, but in weakness, humility, and lowliness. Can you not see the suffering of My heart? Can you not see the love I have for you? Do you not see how I humble Myself before you and how I came to fulfil the righteousness of the Scriptures? I came as a small child in meekness and humility, the one who was anointed as prophet, priest, and king. I came to be like you in your humanity. I came to wash your feet. Would you like to humble yourselves before Me?"

(Turku, Finland, 1996).

Isaiah 40:28–31; Matthew 5:17, 11:29; John 13:3–10; Hebrews 10:39; Revelation 1:6

My Anointing

Our choice

"Do you receive My anointing? Do you know what it means? Do you know what it costs to follow Me? I want to pour out a new anointing upon you now that you have seen a glimpse of My heavenly Kingdom. Leave behind the wounds and expectations that have hindered you. As you come to the cross, I will show you more and more. Because I love you, I want you to choose. I would like you to receive My anointing no matter what it costs"

(Åland, Finland, 1995).

Hebrews 12:1–2; 1 John 2:20

4. JESUS LOOKS FOR OUR RESPONSE

Our Cries

A call to stand firm

"**A**re you prepared to go on with Me? Are you prepared to be faithful? Remember, hindrances cannot be overcome with human strength. Keep firm and stand on My promises. Do not throw away your trust and faith. The pressures that you are under are nothing compared to the glory to be revealed to you. Do not walk like others—dependent on more programs. Move into a new liberty"

(Heiligenstadt, Germany, 1997).

2 Corinthians 4:17; 2 Corinthians 12:9–10, 13:4; Hebrews 10:35

An answer to worry

"I have called you to be worshipers, not worriers. I took your troubles and burdens; I took them on My shoulders on the cross, and you are truly free. It is a gift from Me. If you set your heart on Me and worship Me, you will see My hand upon you and all whom you cherish. Worship Me with a light heart and a joyful spirit. Come into My presence and have fellowship with Me. Lay down everything and learn to be My bride. Do not look to the left or to the right but enter into a new obedience, and anointing, and a new faith and life. Do not look back. I am with you always"

(Niedenstein, Germany, 1999).

Proverbs 4:27; Isaiah 30:21; Matthew 28:20; 1 Peter 2:24

Our Heart

A heart permeated by His fragrance

"I love you with an everlasting love, and I am drawing you with cords of lovingkindness. I am drawing you into My holiness so that you might express My love to others in a deeper measure. Through suffering, I am stripping the deadness from your lives and washing you clean from the influence of the world. I am taking away your hearts of stone and giving you hearts of flesh. The fragrance of My presence in your lives will permeate everything. I will speak mysteries into your hearts, and you will be a reflection of My holiness and My love"

(Ashburnham Place, UK, 1999).

Jeremiah 31:3; Ezekiel 36:25–26; 2 Corinthians 2:15–16; 1 Thessalonians 5:23

Deep Calls to Deep

Do not look for answers, but look to Me

"I came among you born of a woman. I was mocked, despised, spat upon; I came among you to give you My life. Why do you seek for position and recognition? Follow in My footsteps. Trust Me. I have a lot of things to sort out in your hearts. They are cluttered up; your imaginations run riot; and your expectations are unreal. But if your hearts are towards Me, I can begin. I know you want answers. What good are answers unless you know Me? Instead, look to Me and trust Me"

(Ashburnham Place, UK, 1997).

Isaiah 53:3–4; Matthew 18:1–5, 23:5–12; 1 John 3:2–3

Submit and Surrender

Walking together in light

"Why do you always try to keep Me in a box? For freedom I have set you free, and now I ask for permission to work in your life. Do you really realize how precious you are in My sight, each one of you? I made you exactly the person that you are, and I made you beautiful and acceptable. I have a work for you to do. Do you want to do it your way or My way? Surrender your hearts to Me, and I will live fully in you. I know you have many questions and all you can think of are your problems. Am I not bigger than your problems? In My light, you receive light, and that light is the light of the world. You are part of that light to the world. I have touched you, and I will continue to minister My love to you as you minister your love to Me. Come, let us walk together"

(Ashburnham Place, UK, 2001).

Matthew 5:14; John 8:12; Romans 6:13; Galatians 2:20; Galatians 5:1; 1 John 1:7

The path to purification

"Learn to trust Me more. It grieves Me to see how My people fluctuate from being enthusiastic to being despondent and listless. Many things are still born of self, not by My Spirit. Every one of your circumstances is an opportunity to trust in Me. I am drawing you close to me through your difficulties. I am waiting for you to let go of all your fears and to allow Me to purify you. Let Me prepare you to be a beautiful bride one step at a time, one day at a time"

(Sydney, Australia, 2007).

Proverbs 3:5–6; John 15:5; 1 John 1:7–9, 3:2; Revelation 19:7

Dying to Self

Release of My fragrance

"Some of you will suffer because of My Name and be crushed like flowers to produce a wonderful fragrance. I am preparing your hearts. As your days, so shall your strength be. This is a free gift of My love. You will bring many into My kingdom. Do not be afraid of what you are going to suffer because I have already suffered for you. Fear not—you will be comforted"

(Åland, Finland, 1995).

Deuteronomy 33:25; Isaiah 51:12a; Matthew 24:6–7;
Revelation 2:10

Do not be concerned about the cost

"You have come to seek Me. As you behold Me, I will draw you to Myself. I will fulfill your heart's desire to be fruitful. Do not be concerned about the cost. As I was filled with joy in going to the cross, so I will fill you with joy in return for everything you have laid down to follow Me. I am calling you to be among those who prepare the way for My coming. Thank you for laying down your life for Me"

(Enzen, Germany, 2003).

Isaiah 57:14; Hebrews 12:1–2

From doubt to design

"Do you ever doubt My love, My power, My righteousness, My majesty? Do you ever question My purposes and are you mindful of My glory? Are you willing to put aside your wish to be known, to lead your life as you desire? Or will you let Me be the Lord of your life to fill you with My Holy Spirit every minute of the day? Are you willing to die to self for Me?"

(Canberra, Australia, 1992).

Galatians 2:20; Ephesians 5:18

Freedom

Released into relationship

"Why do you carry that old problem around with you? You have prayed about it, but you have never let it go. How can I pour out My love upon you while your face is clouded by problems? Give your problems to Me once and for all. Then you will be free—free to see My face, free to hear My voice, and free to have a more intimate relationship with Me. This is My gift to you. Come, receive it."

(Åland, Finland, 2004).

Psalm 36:10; Philippians 4:6–7

Receive My freedom

"I have come to set the captives free. I have come to break every bond that has held My people. You will know what true liberty is in Me. You will know the purpose of your life. I am unlocking doors to open the way before you. Do not look at yourself, your circumstances, or at your past. I will change you into My likeness. It will be uncomfortable at first, but it will bring you new life as you worship Me. My Spirit will do a glorious work in you. Come, My bride, I want to pour out My love and freedom upon you"

(Amden, Switzerland, 2002).

Luke 4:18; 1 Corinthians 16:9; 2 Corinthians 3:17–18

Walk and Follow

Unencumbered

"Do you want to know Me with a true understanding of who I am? Do you want to follow Me wherever I lead you? Then lay down your burdens and learn to live with a heavenly perspective. How else can you understand My mind and My heart? You are created in My likeness, and you are destined to reflect My life. My heavenly perspective will enable you to overcome all your trials while here on earth. Come and follow Me, and I will teach you"

(Franklin, North Carolina, 1999).

Genesis 1:27; 2 Corinthians 3:18; Colossians 3:2–3

Sanctify Yourself

Called into the fire

"I am separating and sanctifying My people, setting you free from the world. For some, this means pain, but this is from Me because I love you. You shall be a holy people moved only by Me and My Word, not by circumstances, the opinions of others, the winds of doctrine, or the powers of darkness, but only by My Spirit. I will lead you through the fire. Stay with Me, and I will lead you to victory. Let Me cover you with My wings. I am your security. There is no other like Me"

(Schlossau, Germany, 1995).

Psalm 91:4; Isaiah 43:2; Zechariah 4:6; 2 Timothy 2:21

Burning yet not consumed

"I have come to cleanse you in the same way that gold is purified. Look to My cross every day, and I will burn your self-righteousness away. Put everything aside that is secondary in your life until there is nothing left of your own strength, but only that which is of My Spirit"

(Åland, Finland, 2002).

Zechariah 4:6; 1 Peter 1:6–9

Fiery love

"Do not be afraid of My all-consuming fire. It purifies your hearts and is part of My love for you. I want you to burn with passion for Me and for the souls of others. How I long for this fire to burn in your hearts"

(Amden, Switzerland, 2002).

Hebrews 9:13–14; 1 Peter 1:6–9, 22; 1 John 3:3

Kings and Priests

Called into royalty

"I have called you that you might be kings and priests unto Me. You shall be part of My ministry to rule, yes, to rule by prayer, to release My people from the influences of the kingdom of darkness. My time draws near, and I am coming to gather My people. I am coming to gather My elect. I am calling those who will intercede with Me to make it possible for My Spirit to move among the nations"

(Canberra, Australia, 1992).

1Timothy 2:1–2; Revelation 1:6, 5:10

Obedient – not hindered

"Before My throne, you will find rest and peace. Before My throne, you will find tranquillity. Before My throne, every care and every need shall be met. Yet I see My people going astray. Together with your praises and worship, lace your life with dedication, love, and obedience to My will and purpose for this earth. You are called My ambassadors, and so you are. You are royalty among mankind. You wear a scarlet sash bought with My blood. How I yearn that My people will place Me in their hearts so that My glory can be seen among the nations. Search your hearts to see if there is anything there that hinders your royal call"

(Franklin, North Carolina, 1999).

1 Chronicles 28:9; Psalm 57:11; Jeremiah 17:10; Malachi 1:11; John 14:23; 2 Corinthians 5:20; 1 Peter 2:5–9

Deep Calls to Deep

I have chosen you

"You did not choose Me. I chose you. I have chosen you to be kings and priests who offer Me sacrifices of praise and adoration, which rest as a sweet fragrance on My throne, acceptable to our Father. Inherit your royal priesthood. Be bold. This is your calling. Your praise and thanksgiving are like jewels presented before My throne. I cherish your sacrifice of love. As you worship Me, I send angels to do battle on your behalf. Fear not. Come each day and worship Me with real freedom, and I will teach you to live in your priestly role"

(Amden, Switzerland, 2003).

John 15:16; Ephesians 1:4; 2 Corinthians 3:12; 1 Peter 2:4–5, 9.

Songs in the Spirit

These words are the interpretation of the love songs that were received through His Spirit.

Love songs of Jesus

"Put your hand in Mine and do not take it away. Take My arm and let us walk together, and do not turn aside. My love is for you yesterday, today, and tomorrow. It never varies; it is always the same. Put your hand in Mine and never let Me go. I am your lover. I want to ravish you with My love. I do not just want a little of you; I want all of you! Keep your eyes on Mine. Look into My face. Put your hand in Mine. I will never let you go!"

(Sydney, Australia, 2001).

Deuteronomy 28:14; Song of Songs 4:9–10; Isaiah 41:13; Micah 6:8; Hebrews 13:8

"Let me reassure you that I love you. I have prepared a place for you. Enter into what I have for you. I have provided a place of peace, and joy, and rest. So come. Do not be afraid. Come. I will lead you and guide you. This song I have prepared for you is a song of hope!"

(Amden, Switzerland, 2001).

Hosea 2:15; John 16:13; Colossians 1:27

"Did I not sing a love song over you? Do you not remember that I am your bridegroom? I am your Lord but also your lover. I am longing for My bride to prepare her heart before Me and come into the embrace of My love without any fear. Come; rush into My arms with great freedom. This is My heart's desire"

(Horschof, Germany, 2005).

Isaiah 54:5, 62:3–5; Hosea 2:20; Zephaniah 3:17

Deep Calls to Deep

A song of Jesus's victory

"Why are you so anxious? I want to bring you into a new place of liberty and freedom, free from your structures and patterns. Trust Me to set you free. I want to give you My new song—a song that will bring down strongholds in your life. My victory on the cross allows you to sing My songs. There are great victories to be won, born out of My song. Come, I will teach you to sing"

(Amden, Switzerland, 2004).

Exodus 15:2; Psalm 28:7, 32:7, 42:8; John 8:32, 36; Romans 12:2; 2 Corinthians 10:3–5; Philippians 4:6–7; Colossians 2:15

5. THE DAYS AHEAD

My Body

Humble and authentic

"I am releasing a mighty power on the earth; not a power that the world understands, but a power in line with My character. I am nurturing a powerful people of humility and reality—a people with the humility of Moses and the reality of David, a people who see things through My eyes, who will see no barriers to My love for their brothers and sisters, a people who see the hearts of men and women as I see them and who have the humility to help conform this world to My will and My wisdom. I am raising up a people of power who will rule on the earth in reality"

(Canberra, Australia, 1992).

Psalm 133:1–3; Matthew 28:18–20; John 13:34–35; Colossians 2:10; Hebrews 4:12

My authority, My way

"The day is coming when I will indeed be head of My church. You will be My voice, and the world will see Me, not a church organization. No one will take My glory. My servants will be humble and broken and will not want any recognition for themselves. They will be hidden from the world, but will have all My authority. Do you see where you are now? You are walking in the foothills with mountains all around. You are destined to climb the highest mountain. I am bringing My people together. It will be painful because no kingdom of man will stand in My sight. All around the mountains, there are many people hearing My voice. Look for the pathway that I will show you as you climb. Be encouraged; you are on the way"

(Strittmatt, Germany, 1999).

Micah 4:1–2, 6:8 John 17:18; Colossians 1:18, 3:3

Reflection without distortion

"Only as My body gazes at Me does it grow straight, just as a flower grows straight as it reaches for the sun. If My body does not focus on Me, distortions occur. It reflects Me inaccurately, like a mirror with a distorted surface. As you focus on Me, you grow in the right direction"

(Ashburnham Place, UK, 1999).

2 Corinthians 3:18; Hebrews 12:1–2, 11–15

Watered by My Spirit

"I am sounding bells of freedom for you. I am refreshing you and the land with rivers of living water from My Spirit. I am opening old and new fountains. I am watering the desert from below and above. I will give My Spirit without measure and increase will occur where you do not expect it"

(Schlossau, Germany, 1995).

Jeremiah 31:25; Zechariah 13:1; John 3:34, 7:38; Acts 2:17–18

Let go

"I am the Lord who sanctifies and heals you. Let go of relationships and the things that have bound you unrighteously; let go of the things you still hold in your hands. Let go of successes, past glory, deceptions, and disappointments. Do not wait for some moment later; let go now. I will give you the new for the old as you let go. I will give you a new, soft heart. Are you ready? Only then can I give you all I have"

(Schlossau, Germany, 1995).

Exodus 15:26; Isaiah 43:18–19; Ezekiel 36:26; 1 Corinthians 6:11; 1 Peter 5:7

The Nations

Determining the destiny of your nation

"The destiny of your nation is not decided by the government, the economy, or any other means. The earth is Mine and the fullness therein. I have given you authority to decide where your nation is going. Would you come to Me to satisfy your own ambitions or to sit with Me while I open your understanding about how to pray for the deliverance of your nation? I will move in your nation if My people come to Me with a hungry heart and say, 'Lord, here I am. I will sit at Your feet. I will be Your instrument and be obedient to You'"

(Canberra, Australia, 1992).

Psalm 2:8, 24:1; Jeremiah 33:3; Luke 10:38–42; Revelation 2:26

The washing of forgiveness

"Forgiveness is like a rushing mountain stream, sparkling in the sun and bringing life to all who come to drink its refreshing and cleansing water. Drink the water of forgiveness continually and lead others there so that they can enter into all that the Father wants to give them. I am going to shake the nations. Many things will not be important anymore. Be prepared for My holiness"

(Herrnhut, Germany, 1998).

Haggai 2:7; Hebrews 12:14; Matthew 6:14–15; Colossians 3:13

Deep Calls to Deep

My song of love over the nations

"Hear the trumpet calling deep in your spirit. Hear it on the mountains; hear it in the valleys, all across the nations, all across the earth. The trumpet calls of My love to all nations and to every tribe. Answer the call, My people. Come home to the place prepared for you in My love"

(Ashburnham Place, UK, 1999).

Joel 2:1; Matthew 24:31; John 14:2–3

My love for the nations

"My heart cries out to the nations. My song goes out across the waters, and My Spirit moves across the face of the earth, touching the hearts of men, crying to them, 'Return to Me.' In these last days, I am calling and separating out of the nations a people who will give themselves wholly to Me, a people who will allow themselves to be cleansed, purified, sanctified, and prepared, who will take their stand for holiness. I am asking My people, 'Whom shall I send? Who will go for Me? Who will sing My song and proclaim My Word to the nations? Who will pay the price? Who will surrender wholeheartedly to the power of My love?' I will transform those who respond to reflect My glory. The beauty and fragrance of My Son will flow from them. There will be rivers of living water, and wherever there is barrenness and death, life shall spring forth. The revival of nations will be based on surrender, humility, and commitment to holiness"

(Ashburnham Place, UK, 1999).

Joel 2:12; Psalm 105:1; Isaiah 6:8; Mark 16:15; 2 Corinthians 2:15–16; Ephesians 5:25–27; Revelation 7:9–10, 22:1

My prevailing purpose for the nations

"My purposes are being fulfilled in the earth, even as nation rises against nation. I have taken My stand, and I will see how the nations respond to My Word. All things shall be placed under My feet. Evil will prevail in many places. See what I do and follow Me. This will be a difficult time as I test the hearts of people to see if they will glorify Me. Pay attention to My Word as you have never done before. I am with you"

(Caloundra, Australia, 1999).

Deuteronomy 8:2; Matthew 24:5–7, 28:20; John 5:19–20; Hebrews 2:8

My glorious healing in the nations

"I will send you out two by two. I will send you out across the land. I will lead you where you are to go. Do not plan it yourself. I will go before you. You will be visiting with empty hands but with a heart full of compassion, love, and mercy for all the people of the land. As you go, I will open doors and create situations where you will be instruments of My grace. Sometimes, there will be surprises. As you obey Me, I will do glorious things in the hearts of people and bring much reconciliation and healing in the land. I will stir up again the desire for people to seek Me, and they will find Me. Be sensitive and obedient when I call you, even when you do not understand. Trust Me; that is all that I ask of you because the work of healing is Mine alone"

(Enzen, Germany, 2004).

Deuteronomy 31:8; Psalm 32:8; Jeremiah 29:12–14; Mark 6:7–8

Missions

Be ready to go when I call

"I want to guide you in a new way, step by step. The time of narrowness is over. I will put you on top of spiritual mountains to sing songs of deliverance and to be watchmen to change the nation. I will send you out to the left and the right; I am preparing you. Be ready to go to the highest places and to the deepest valleys. Listen for the call of My Spirit and go when you hear Me. I speak freedom and deliverance for My people and freedom in every nation"

(Niedenstein, Germany, 1999).

Psalm 32:7; Isaiah 54:2, 62:6; 2 Corinthians 3:17

Will you follow Me?

"You cry out for your land. Are you ready for Me to send you wherever I choose? Are you ready to speak with boldness while people laugh at you? Are you ready? My eyes are looking for a people who will follow Me and not waiver. I am preparing a people to follow Me through the hills, and valleys, and the cities. Will you be amongst them? Now is the time to prepare your hearts. Now is the time to lay down the idols that I reveal in your life. Now is the time for Me to train you to love Me with all your heart, and mind, and all that is within you. Will you follow Me? Wherever I send you, I will never leave you. I am your light and strength"

(Neidenstein, Germany, 1999).

Psalm 27:1; Matthew 4:19, 8:20, 22:37; Ephesians 6:19

Deep Calls to Deep

I will send you to islands

"I have chosen you amongst many, making you strong arrows. I am putting you into My bow, and I will send you to islands, to the cold lands, and to the hot lands. I will send you to the many and to the few. Others will say, 'Come,' but you must hear My voice because they want you for themselves, and not for My Kingdom. I send you not only to reflect My glory but also for a deeper work—to bring unity. Go where I send you. Stay until I call you back"

(Ashburnham Place, UK, 1999).

Matthew 28:19; Mark 16:15

The Battle

Preparing your hearts for battle

"I am gathering My army across the earth to battle the forces of darkness. Now is the time to prepare your heart under My sovereignty. Prepare your mind, heart, and spirit, and quicken your footsteps after Me. We are at the beginning, and there is much work to be done. Gird up your loins, for the battle will be strong. Let Me lead you so that you will be able to withstand the enemy. I am the Captain of the Hosts, and I will train you day by day if you will submit to Me. My loved ones, the victory is Mine"

(Pietermaritzburg, South Africa, 1996).

Joshua 5:13–15; Ephesians 6:10–18; Revelation 19:11–14

Deep Calls to Deep

Vanquishing the enemy

"I want to show you new ways to do battle based on the cross. As you live the life of the cross, the enemy is totally defeated because I overcame him at Calvary. I am drawing My people closer to Me to show them victorious ways of living"

(Heiligenstadt, Germany, 1997).

Ephesians 6:10–19; Colossians 2:13–15, 3:1–3

Do not let the enemy rob you

"Dark storm clouds are forming over your land. I am coming with My mighty power, coming with My trumpet call. My people are being raised in every part of this land among those who have been sitting with Me, those who hear My voice. Be encouraged; it takes time to prepare their hearts while a mighty army is being assembled. Stay in My peace and rest. Do not let the enemy rob you of what you have received from Me"

(Heiligenstadt, Germany, 1997).

Joel 2:1–2; John 10:11, 20:21

Your Inheritance

Rise up

"When the morning star rises in your hearts, I am there waiting for you. Rise up into the heavenly realms. This is your inheritance and your dwelling place. That is where you will hear My voice. As the dawn comes, rise up. Let us dwell together and work together. Do not be disturbed by the things going on among you. Fix your eye on Me. Be focused on Me alone. I am your Redeemer; I have conquered the evil one. I give you the power to live a conqueror's life. It is your inheritance; possess it"

(Enzen, Germany, 2001).

Ephesians 2:6; Hebrew 12:1–2; 1 John 5:4; 2 Peter 1:18–21; Revelation 2:28

Taste and see

"Taste and see that I am good. I am bringing you into a new land— your inheritance in My kingdom. I have your life in My hands. I will lead you into the new life of peace and tranquillity. Picture a clear blue sky with not a cloud to be seen; the air is pure and crisp, and the earth is green and at peace, and the countryside is in harmony with My Spirit. Can you imagine the scene? Can you see it? Then why do you disturb the picture? Do not let darkness come in. Do not let the vultures fly. Take your inheritance. Possess it; it is yours. I will lead you into the new life I have prepared for you. I love you deeply with My strong bridegroom love"

(Åland, Finland, 2002).

Psalm 25:1, 34:8; John 14:27

Hope

Returning hope

"I am the God of hope. I will exchange hope for your broken dreams, expectations, and visions. Receive hope from Me. I will set you free and fill you from My riches in glory. I will strengthen your faith. There will be no more wavering. Stand firm, filled with hope, faith, and love"

(Schlossau, Germany, 1995).

Isaiah 41:10; Jeremiah 29:11; Romans 15:13; 1 Corinthians 13:13, 16:13–14; Ephesians 1:18; Philippians 4:19

My Joy

Come quickly

"Come to Me quickly. I will give you peace and rest and strengthen you to make your burdens light. Receive this rest and joy and impart it to others. They will come to you because you have My joy and peace"

(Åland, Finland, 1995).

Matthew 11:28; John 14:27; Hebrews 12:2

Complete oneness

"You belong to Me. With Me, your soul is safe because you have given your life to Me. You are hidden with Me in God. This is the truth. See the true value of being hidden in Me. See that the world has no lasting value for you. You make My joy complete as I am in you and you are in Me. As you desire these things, you will find your security in Me"

(Ashburnham Place, UK, 2003).

Colossians 3:1–11

My Glory

Shining from the inside

"You will take My glory wherever you set your feet, and many will come into My Kingdom. I will send you to foreign lands. You will sleep in places where you would never dream of going. Walk the way of the Lamb. Desire the lowly way, which is the way of true power, victory, joy, and freedom. Take the fresh waters from My fountain and, like the children of Israel, eat the manna that I give you fresh each day. Be faithful unto death, and I will give you the crown of victory"

(Schlossau, Germany, 1995).

Mark 16:15; John 17:22; Revelation 2:10; 2 Corinthians 4:5; 1 Peter 4:14

Deep Calls to Deep

The shining One

"In the twinkling of an eye, you will be changed. This is your destiny. For now, you are on earth to reflect the glory of My Son. My heart cries for My people to reflect My Son's glory. It is more important than all the other things that you do for Me. If your heart is willing, I will change you from one degree of glory to another to reflect My Son"

(Amden, Switzerland, 2000).

John 17:22–24; 1 Corinthians 15:52; 2 Corinthians 3:18, 4:3–6

PART THREE

POISED FOR MORE

In this end-time harvest, it is more important than ever to bring people to sit at the feet of Jesus. In His presence, they will find a never-ending source of living water and have the opportunity to dedicate their hearts and lives to Him. As members of the body of Christ, we all have the privilege of tapping into the reproductive promise of Hebrews 6:14, "Surely in blessing I will bless you, and in multiplying I will multiply you."

As we recall the many gatherings we attended, we can identify eight themes that were emphasized time and again by the Holy Spirit: Beholding His Glory, Bridal Love, The Ministry of the Holy Spirit, Dying to Self, Entering His Rest, Waiting on the Lord, The Place of Prayer, and The Song of the Lord. We have summarized some of the important points from these themes, trusting that they will help you to grow into a more intimate relationship with Jesus.

We encourage you to recognize that the Spirit of God is always moving and wants to reveal even more about Jesus to us. Creation of new life abounds when the Spirit of truth collides with human hearts that are willing and ready to receive Him. Imagine what could happen within our families, our communities, our cities, and our nations if the hovering Spirit was welcomed by more people focused only on one thing: living in the presence of Jesus.

These themes are presented in note form as an encouragement for you to invite the Holy Spirit to sow the seeds of revelation and knowledge into your life—seeds that will inspire and equip you to build your relationship with Jesus. Learning to be "poised for more" is our vision and heart's desire for the growth of the Kingdom of God in your life.

1. BEHOLDING THE LORD AND HIS GLORY

The Bible says, "Now the Lord is the Spirit; and where the Spirit of the Lord is, there is liberty. We all with unveiled face, beholding as in a mirror the glory of the Lord, are being transformed into the same image from glory to glory, just as by the Spirit of the Lord" (2 Corinthians 3:17–18). It is the sovereign work of the Holy Spirit to progressively transform us into Jesus's image through increasing revelations of His nature and His presence. The Holy Spirit longs to teach us to walk in the fullness of our liberty. As we walk in repentance with an unveiled face, we are able to gaze at Jesus Himself. In doing so, we see not only His grace and His works, but we can look into His face and see and know the altogether lovely One and His character, as revealed in His Word.

To behold Jesus with an unveiled face means that we need to be sure that there is nothing blocking our communication with Him and our Father. We need to come with our minds renewed, our spirit open, and with a cleansed and purified heart free of the influence of the world, the flesh, and the Devil. Then the image of Jesus can be imprinted deeply upon us.

In the stillness of learning to behold the Lord, our minds find it difficult to grasp that anything beneficial can occur. However, the scriptures assure us that as we behold the glory of the Lord, we will be transformed into the same image. This doesn't happen all at once. Beholding the glory of the Lord involves focusing on His power and life, His honor, and His excellence. It forms our perspective of Him. It is the Holy Spirit who does the transformation. Let us take the opportunity to consider Jesus in all His beauty, in all His glory, and in every area of His work and His character as revealed in His Word.

The Bible also says, "Therefore having this ministry by the mercy of God we do not lose heart" (2 Corinthians 4:1). What ministry are we talking about here? The ministry of beholding the glory of the Lord and of reflecting this glory. We do not realize how powerful it is to reflect the glory of the Lord when we have been with Him. The following Word should encourage us: "We possess this precious treasure of the divine light of the gospel in frail human vessels that the greatness of the power may be from God and not from ourselves" (2 Corinthians 4:6–7). We need to be filled and transformed by the Holy Spirit to behold the glory of Jesus and mirror His character to others.

2. BRIDAL LOVE

"**Y**ou shall love the Lord your God with all your heart, with all your soul and with all your mind" (Matthew 22:37–39). This is a lifelong pursuit that must not be overlooked by our everyday busy-ness in doing good works for Him. Many other things prevent us from falling deeply in love with Jesus; for example, holding back from Him due to circumstances that have hurt us in the past or wanting to keep our independence in specific areas of our lives. We can learn to keep the greatest commandment when we grasp two vital things. First, that the love of Christ has been poured out upon us and we have become part of His living body. Second, we are betrothed to Jesus as part of His bride.

The Song of Songs provides a wonderful picture of our lifelong journey to develop a bridal love for Jesus. As we hear Jesus's "lyrics of love" sung over us, our love for Him will blossom. The way our love for Jesus develops is revealed in the three stages of the bride's maturing love for her bridegroom.

In the first stage, the bride declares, "My beloved is mine and I am his" (Song of Songs 2:16). She is thrilled at being in love, but the relationship has not yet gone deep enough that she is aware of her faults, her subtle sin, which is like little foxes that spoil the vine of fruitfulness. It takes time for her to be free of the fears, doubts, and compromises that prevent her from developing a more intimate relationship with her lover. Meanwhile, he waits for her, looking at her with eyes of love, yearning for her love to mature. How important that she spends much time alone with him to fall into a deeper love.

In the second stage, the bride's longing for her bridegroom's love is beginning to flow from the center of her being: "I am my beloved's and my beloved is mine" (Song of Songs 6:3). Now she is learning to delight in her lover—to be open to depending on him and to serving and ministering to him with the fullness of her love.

In the final stage, she joyfully proclaims, "I am my beloved's and his desire is towards me" (Song of Songs 7:10). She has forgotten about herself, and her identity is now totally wrapped up in her love for the bridegroom.

The three stages lead to a rich season of fruitfulness (Song of Songs 7:11–13), with the bride and bridegroom going forward into the world bonded together in lifelong love.

This "song" opens the way for each one of us to run into the arms of Jesus, our bridegroom, Lord, and lover. He is ready to draw us to Himself. He waits to hear our questing voice: "My beloved is Mine and I am His." How essential it is to dwell in this place of growing intimacy. We must take time to allow Him to transform us step by step into being His bride as He passionately proclaims: "You have ravished my heart ... with one look of your eyes" (Song of Songs 4:9). He waits to bring us into the depths of His love, declaring, "I am overcome by your love, My bride." The Lord is longing for His bride to be ready to rule with Him as He presents her, a glorious church, to our Father. How vital it is for

each one of us to seek after Jesus continually, thirsting for the depths of His love.

During our last gathering in Horschof, Germany, Jesus shared this intimate word with the group:

> "Come each one of you; come and draw close to Me. There is nothing to stop you coming close to Me into the embrace of My arms. I am waiting to draw you closer and closer to My heart. Did I not sing a love song over you? Do you not remember that I am your bridegroom? I am your Lord but also your lover, and I am longing for My bride to prepare her heart before Me and come into the embrace of My love without any fear. Come; rush into My arms with great freedom. This is My heart's desire. Did you hear My love song to you? Did you receive the song of My love for you, My bride?"

3. THE MINISTRY OF THE HOLY SPIRIT

The Holy Spirit is waiting to bestow His gifts on us and open up the Word to minister Jesus's life to us. This He did constantly through the gift of prophecy. During most of our gatherings, it took several days for the Holy Spirit to bring us to the place of flowing together, to be in one accord and so discern what was foremost on Jesus's heart. At times, we had to be careful not to presume what His next move would be. Otherwise, we ran the risk of overlooking a word for us, or response from us, that was important to Jesus.

When the Holy Spirit had liberty to minister to our hearts, He did unexpected things, often pinpointing unresolved issues. Sometimes, He showed individuals how much "baggage" they were carrying and patiently led them to lay down all that is not truly born of the Spirit. The Spirit knows the hindrances and anxieties that rob us of peace and the ability to focus solely on Jesus. He delivers us from past bondages and present-day worries.

A manifestation of this work of the Holy Spirit occurred in Finland, when a woman realized that she still had a spirit of rebellion. Her problem began as a teenager when she rebelled against her parents' authority. She placed a poster of a rock singer on the outside of her bedroom door and continually sang his songs, which were written to sow seeds of rebellion among the youth. During a time of worship one morning, she realized that this rebellious spirit had invaded her own family. Under the Holy Spirit's conviction, she wept in deep confession and repentance. As the Holy Spirit ministered Jesus's healing love to her, she knew that she was freely forgiven. Her face became radiant, and she saw her true role as a God-fearing mother.

Many people attending a time of sitting at Jesus's feet had little appreciation of the importance of the Holy Spirit's gifts (1 Corinthians 12:7–11 and 14:1–5), together with the gifts of the Father (Romans 12:3–8), and the gifts of Jesus (Ephesians 4:7–16). Many church congregations have been living on a starvation diet, relying only on church programs to meet their needs. The practical, sanctifying work of the Holy Spirit in our inner lives is essential. By surrendering to the Holy Spirit and letting Him continually renew our minds, we will grow more and more into Jesus's likeness (Romans 8:14–15, 12:2) and bear the rich fruit of the Spirit (Galatians 5:22–24). The Holy Spirit delights to glorify Jesus and to make known to us the fullness of our inheritance as the sons and daughters of God.

4. DYING TO SELF

This is the battle of all battles. Will we, or will we not, devote ourselves entirely to Jesus? If we are to be His disciples, we must sacrifice everything to this single purpose. Paul sums it up: "I have been crucified with Christ. It is no longer I who live but Christ lives in me and the life which I now live in the flesh, I live by faith in the Son of God who loved me and gave Himself for me" (Galatians 2:20).

At first, in the joy of pardon, we want to live for Christ and trust in His help. We are largely ignorant of the terrible enmity of the flesh against God. However, the fallen nature of our body and soul exerting their power over us refuse to let the Spirit alone lead us (Romans 8:4–7). Only the bitter experience of failure to follow Jesus in the way we know we should stirs us to know Him better (Romans 7:19–20).

We need to give intelligent consent, by an act of our will, to die with Christ and so be a partaker of His life. Our human nature ("self") battles to give up its will, and this hinders God's work. The essence of sin is living independently of God, refusing to let God take control over all of our circumstances. Unless self is replaced by the life of Christ, it is impossible to abide in Him (John 15:3–8).

We need to realize that self is not dead, but we are dead to self. When we listen to self, it will control us. We give power to self through ignorance, a lapse in watchfulness, or unbelief (Romans 6:5–11; 2 Corinthians 5:14–15). When Jesus takes the place of self, He leads us into the peace and grace of the new life. When we are dead to our old human nature, a wonderful transformation occurs. The Lord's protection fully clothes us, and we are hidden with Christ in God. Dying to self enables us to naturally set our minds on the things above, not the things on earth (Colossians 3:1–3). As we embrace the concept of dying to self, it becomes a grace, not a duty. We are free to accept His total responsibility for our lives; that is when Satan is restrained from having access to us.

What does "dying to self" mean in practical terms? It involves the surrender of our rights, our wills, our emotions and those things that control our minds (Luke 14:26).

This goes against the culture of Western societies because we are trained to claim and protect our rights. We must be set free from our own self-righteousness, self-justification, and self-sufficiency, all of which are rooted in pride and arrogance. Instead of measuring ourselves with our own yardsticks, we should always use the true standard of God's Word.

In the midst of this daily battle, we cannot always see that the Holy Spirit is constantly guiding us to die to self to reveal the life of Christ given to us. Let us remember that "we always carry around in our body the death of Jesus so that the life of Jesus may be revealed in our body. For we who live are constantly being delivered over to death for Jesus's sake, so that the life of Jesus may be manifested in our mortal flesh. So death works in us, but life in you" (2 Corinthians 4:8–12).

The fruit of dying to self is that a new depth of life arises within us, along with a new depth of love. We are flooded with grace, our minds are enlightened with divine light, and our wills grow with the fire of divine love. We need to keep Jesus's challenge ever before us: "If anyone desires to come after Me, let him deny himself and take up his cross and follow Me. For whoever desires to save his life will lose it, but whoever loses his life for My sake will find it" (Matthew 16:24–25).

5. ENTERING HIS REST

This is one of the great secrets of our Christian life: "There remains, therefore, a rest for the people of God, for he who has entered His rest has himself ceased from his works, as God did from His" (Hebrews 4:9–10). God's rest is a gift that imparts His stability and peace to us. Through the grace and peace of His rest, we become relaxed people, even during trials. God's rest enables us to stand like a rock against the onslaught of the enemy.

It is one thing to believe in and desire the Lord's rest: it is another to give Him permission to bring us into His rest. The Lord is the only one who can help us cease from our strivings and enter His rest. Our role is to demonstrate that He has our permission by pursuing His rest diligently.

Each day, we need to find a place where we can be renewed spiritually, physically, and emotionally. In other words, we need to make time to be alone with Jesus in the "secret place." We also need to enjoy a Sabbath rest each week; this is God's order for our lives. When we rest in this way, we will bear more fruit than those who labor seven days a week. When we are in His rest, our faith life and our prayer life are interwoven, enabling our spirit to be in continuous communion with Jesus, whatever our circumstances. From a place of rest, we can draw near to the throne of grace with confidence and hear what is on the heart of God (Hebrews 4:16).

We need to expect the outcome of our deepening rest and the stilling of our souls is to be joined to the calm of heaven. Rest and quietness are the foundations of revival because it is when we are at rest that we can hear the still, small voice of the Lord giving us instructions on how to meet the spiritual needs of other people. Once we have entered the rest of God, there are several things that we need to do to stay there.

First, we must continue to lean on Him in absolute trust, exchanging our self-reliance for His rest. This will enable God to work out that which is right, bringing glory to His name in all our circumstances.

Second, we must be transparent in every area of our lives. When we bring every thought, imagination, argument, and speculation captive to obey Christ (2 Corinthians 10:3–6), we acquire new eyes and see things from His perspective. By being completely honest with God, we not only live in rest and liberty, but we are changed into His likeness (2 Corinthians 3:16–18).

Third, we must depend on His Word, for "the Word of God is living and powerful and sharper than any two-edged sword, piercing as far as the division of soul and spirit and able to judge the thoughts and intents of the heart" (Hebrews 4:12). When we allow His Word to penetrate our lives, it teaches us true discernment and brings healing and rest.

6. WAITING ON THE LORD

S ome people find it difficult to know how to wait on God; others think it is somewhat of a mystery. The Bible repeatedly encourages us to wait on God and explains what this involves.

Learning to wait on Him while in His rest is a foundation of our walk with God—an expression of our complete trust in Him. In the age of the Internet, we are accustomed to wanting instant answers. God operates at a different pace. If we become impatient, we run the risk of substituting our thoughts, our words, scriptures we know, or prophecies we have heard to fill the void. Instead, we need to wait until He takes the initiative to speak to us in whatever way He wishes.

God Himself is our role model. He waits so that He can be gracious to us even in our times of willfulness (Isaiah 30:18). Jesus is also waiting until His enemies are made His footstool (Hebrews 10:12–13).

We need to learn to wait on God in two ways: to wait *on* Him by simply being content to be in His presence and to wait *for* Him by adopting an attitude that accepts that His timing is perfect. Let us remember that "The Lord is good to those who wait for Him, to the soul who seeks Him. It is good that one should hope and wait quietly for the salvation of the Lord" (Lamentations 3:25–26). As a woman waits for the birth of her baby, we also need to be patient while God brings His purposes to fruition in our lives. During such times, we can deepen our love relationship with Jesus, just as a husband and wife can grow closer while anticipating the arrival of their child.

When the Holy Spirit sows a seed in our hearts, we can do nothing to make it happen except watch and wait for Him to bring it to pass. As a farmer waits for the harvest after sowing his seed, so, too, we must wait for the fruition of our prayers. Forecasting the way God will answer our prayers is not helpful; instead, we should wait in expectant hope. Meditating on the words that we receive from God helps us to focus on Him while we wait. In doing so, we will learn new dimensions of God's character as we observe how He fulfills the promises in His Word. Let God's purposes be woven into every area of our lives by the Holy Spirit, teaching us what it means to wait for, watch, wonder at, and then witness His infinite love and care at work. Waiting means standing under the shadow of the Almighty in strength, enduring until the answer comes.

7. THE PLACE OF PRAYER

M any of the people who joined us to sit at the feet of Jesus had different ways of praying. Sometimes it was a challenge to pray together. We had to let go of our set ways so that we could be guided by the Word and the Holy Spirit. Jesus wanted to show us how to still our hearts so that they would naturally turn to Him in prayer.

All true prayer is conceived in heaven, and God is looking for vessels for these prayers to be birthed here on earth. In our growing relationship with Jesus, we began to understand the yearning He has for us to partner with Him in prayer (Romans 8:25–27). Many times, we were surprised by the directions in which He led us. These involved times of repentance, fresh insights into scripture, songs in the Spirit, the manifestation of various gifts, a cry for mercy for various peoples and nations, and times of entering into powerful declarations of God's Word.

We learned that when the Holy Spirit shows us what is on Jesus's heart for His church and the world, He imparts an ability to us to pray that is beyond our intellectual understanding of the situation—a place where our spirits are constantly tuned into Him and a place where, at the prompting of the Holy Spirit, prayer flows spontaneously through us as we join Him in His response to the prayer need. We come to the place of praying without ceasing (1 Thessalonians 5:17).

On one occasion, He spoke to us through His Word in Jeremiah 6:16, 17: "Stand in the ways and see and ask for the old paths where the good way is and walk in it, then you will find rest for your souls ... Also I set watchmen over you saying, 'Listen to the sound of the trumpet.'" This is a call to hear and obey the Lord in these testing days. It challenges us to live according to His statutes and judgements as well as to stand with Jesus to ask our Father to raise up true prophetic watchmen who will declare to the church, "Build up, build up, clear the way, remove the stumbling block out of the way of the spiritual return of My people" (Isaiah 57:14, Amplified).

We are witnessing the beginnings of Jesus's predictions in Matthew 24. In response, we need to come before the Lord to hear how to pray for God's purposes to be fulfilled among the nations. We have a part to play in prayer to see that the Lord establishes Israel as a prophetic sign to the nations in preparation for Jesus's return. The following two verses are pertinent examples: "For the Lord will not forsake His people for His great name's sake, because it has pleased the Lord to make Israel a people for Himself" (1 Samuel 12:22) and "Blessed be the Lord God of Israel for He has visited and redeemed His people and has raised up a horn of salvation for us in the house of His servant David" (Luke 1:68–69).

We see five priorities for prayer on Jesus's heart for His church and the nations:

- The completion of the great commission (Matthew 28:18–19)
- The bride preparing herself to be ready for the Lord's return (Revelation 19:7–9)

- The veil being lifted from the eyes of the Jewish people to reveal Christ as their Messiah (2 Corinthians 3:13–16; Zechariah 12:10)
- Ministry to the poor (Isaiah 58:6–8)
- The gathering of all nations before the throne of God (Matthew 25:31–32).

8. THE SONGS OF THE LORD

T he Word of God is full of songs, each with its own purpose, encompassing important events from Exodus through Revelation.

Songs in the Old Testament

- Exodus 15 is a strong, vibrant song that Moses and the children of Israel sang after the Egyptians were overthrown in the midst of the sea.
- In 1 Chronicles chapter 16, King David, with Asaph and the Levitical priests, established continuous worship before God, making music on stringed instruments, harps, and trumpets.
- Psalm 137 is a picture of Judah's lament, being mocked as captives in Babylon. "How shall we sing the Lord's song in a foreign land?" They had lost their freedom to worship the Lord because their hearts were chained by their captivity.
- Isaiah 30:29–33 is a song of indignation and warfare against Israel's old entrenched enemies who have led her astray into the depths of depravity.
- Zephaniah 3:14–17 is a song about the promise of restoration for Israel as God embraced her in His quiet love, expressing His faithfulness to forgive and restore His people.

- We are encouraged to sing "with festive praises and with prophetic songs given to us spontaneously by the Spirit" (Colossians 3:16).

- In Ephesians 5:18–21, we are told to "speak to one another in psalms and hymns and spiritual songs, to sing and make melody in our hearts to the Lord."

- 1 Corinthians 14:15 says that we are to sing both in the spirit and with understanding under the guidance of the Holy Spirit in ways that are appropriate to the occasion.

- The prime example of the Lord's song in the New Testament is when Mary greeted Elizabeth. The babe within Elizabeth's womb leapt for joy, and Elizabeth was filled with the Holy Spirit and proclaimed aloud that Mary was blessed among women. Mary responded in song: "My soul magnifies the Lord and my spirit has rejoiced in God my Savior" (Luke 1:39–55).

The songs of the Lord have continued since biblical times. Handel's *Messiah*, a major expression of worship through the centuries, was composed in twenty-four days under an extraordinary anointing. It is an amazing declaration of the Lord's majesty and glory as well as the power of Christ's sacrifice on the cross.

God promises the restoration of all things, which includes the songs of the Lord. As with all the spiritual gifts, the main purpose of the songs of the Lord is to build up His body. We can expect to hear and be edified by new and prophetic songs.

A New Song

In the Psalms, we are exhorted to sing new songs to the Lord and to rejoice in Him with thanksgiving and praise, giving Him the honor and glory due to Him (Psalm 40:3). The Lord delights in giving us new songs during our times of personal worship, as well as in times of corporate worship. He even gives songs in the night (Psalm 42:8). With these, we recognize His prompting as an inner witness (Romans 8:16). The seeds for a song are planted, growing into words and melodies, setting our hearts on fire.

A Prophetic Song

God uses prophetic songs given by the Holy Spirit to communicate His divine purposes. Such songs encourage us at critical times, lifting our hearts in praise and renewing hope. They are like water to thirsty hearts and give us fresh revelations of God's power at work among us, as shown so vividly in Psalm 96.

God raised up Deborah as a prophetess and a warrior whose prophetic song inspired Israel's victory over the Canaanites under Sisera, with his nine hundred chariots of iron (Judges chapter 5). The intercessory song of faith in Habakkuk chapter 3 presents a real challenge to the church, as we see the spirit of Babylon striding across much of the world in these last days.

How we need to receive prophetic songs today, born of the Spirit and flowing out of God's grace and authority—songs of exhortation that inject new life into our hearts and influence His church to grow and multiply, songs that declare the majesty and sovereignty of the Lord over the nations. The day is coming when the songs of the Lord will be sung freely again among us as a mighty chorus resounding across the earth. The powers of darkness cannot prevent the fresh impartation of His songs to His church.

As His Word says, "So we have the prophetic word made more sure, to which you do well to pay attention as to a lamp shining in a dark place, until the day dawns and the morning star arises in your hearts" (2 Peter 1:19).

A FINAL WORD

J esus, seated in His chair in the cloistered courtyard, continues to wait. Have *you* come to the place where you make time with Him your first priority each day? Be assured that each moment at His feet is potentially life transforming. As you wait on Him, He will direct you one day at a time to fulfill your calling, and you will bear abundant fruit for the kingdom.

A final word given at the end of a gathering in Sydney speaks to us all:

> "You have come to set aside time with Me. I am in your midst. I want you to receive new revelations from My Word—new knowledge and a new boldness. What I require is that you give Me first place above all your works so that I can fellowship with you. When I see that your hearts are in the right place, hungering for Me, I will speak. You all have an important part to play, with all your brothers and sisters, in the creation of My tapestry, a tapestry where each stitch and color is in the right place. As you listen to what I am saying to you through each other, I will prepare you for the important days ahead."

PERSPECTIVES FROM PARTICIPATING LEADERS

W e invited a number of the leaders who hosted us in several nations to share what it meant to each one of them personally to spend time sitting at Jesus's feet.

✛ ✛ ✛

After the toughest season in our lives in 1995, my wife, Iris, and I held our first time of "Sitting at the Feet of Jesus" with Noel and Barbara Bell in Schlossau, a little town in the Bavarian forest. As we began to wait before Jesus, He touched me with His Holy Spirit. All the wounds of two years of intense suffering broke out with tears as I confessed my personal bankruptcy to the Lord. I received a deep inner healing. Other leaders also had their hearts healed emotionally. I tried to serve the Lord by hosting the meeting, but He served me. My inner healing remains until today, twenty years after that awesome experience.

Since then, we have met seven times with others and with Noel and Barbara—our spiritual parents—to sit at Jesus's feet. Every gathering was different. Sometimes it took two days to enter fully into His presence. When that occurred, Jesus would reveal Himself in extraordinary ways, opening His treasure chest for us. The richness of the different gifts of the Holy Spirit in words of knowledge and wisdom, visions, and prophecies was amazing. We soon learned to function together as part of the body of Christ. There were spontaneous songs, spiritual eyes and ears were opened, healings and reconciliations occurred, and life-long friendships were formed.

Our gathering in Herrnhut in eastern Germany was of special significance. This is the town where Count Zinzendorf and the Moravians sent missionaries out into the world in the 1700s, and it is a place of great tradition. Through our time of sitting at the feet of Jesus there, God put together some puzzle pieces to release the fresh breath of the Holy Spirit.

God has given Noel and Barbara a special gift in calling the body of Christ to come and sit at Jesus's feet. This should not end with their ministry—it must become a lifestyle.

—Ekkehard and Iris Höfig, founders and pastors
of Immanuel-Gemeinde Nürnberg, Germany

✣ ✣ ✣

Sitting at Jesus's feet is one of the most rewarding adventures we can have as God's people. To spend quality time with Jesus without an agenda is essential; it allows Him to reveal what He has in mind for us. With no speakers or agenda of our own, He has the liberty to move among us to touch us as individuals and as a group.

The first time this happened was on our wedding anniversary in Pretoria, South Africa. While sitting quietly at His feet, Jesus touched our marriage and gave Pauline and me a far deeper love for Him and for each other.

We now make a special time of sitting at Jesus's feet each year. Afterward, people often ask when the next one will be held because they enjoyed the reality of His presence so much. We do not see this as another meeting; it is the event of the year. We would not miss it for anything because time in God's presence is the most valuable time in all the world.

There is no place I would rather be than sitting at Jesus's feet, talking with my heavenly Father. Thank you, Jesus, for making your Father our destination, and thank you, Father, for allowing us to be in Your presence through Jesus, and to be led by Your Holy and liberty-giving Spirit.

—David Tidy, coordinator of Prayer Warriors International,
United Kingdom

✝ ✝ ✝

Sitting at the feet of Jesus has been a foundational principle of Health Care in Christ since we spent a week in 1993 with Noel and Barbara Bell seeking His face for Health Care. We vividly remember worshiping God with high praises while torrential rain pounded on the roof. In a loud voice above the storm, Noel declared a word in a tongue, which was interpreted, "Why do you stand alone?" We were puzzled by His question until we read Luke 10:1-2, which gave us understanding, in part, about what the Lord was saying to us. Luke 10 became our foundational chapter and mission statement for Health Care in Christ. It established our work within a place of intimacy with Him to bring, with compassion and Christ-like care, healing and wholeness to people. Those words received during the storm have resounded through the years as we have networked with other ministries in Health Care. We are very grateful to the Lord for the apostolic mantle that Noel and Barbara have carried in prayer for our nation. We recommend this book to you.

—Ken and Ros Curry, Health Care in Christ, Australia

✠ ✠ ✠

For many of us at the first "Sitting at the Feet of Jesus" session in Franklin, North Carolina, in 1997, it was a life-changing experience. Since that first gathering, many families and young people in various locations near us have also come to sit at Jesus's feet. Some of these precious times occurred on the beautiful Nantahala mountain range while watching eagles. Those involved heard the Lord speak to them and were assured that God loves them and has a plan for their lives. This simple act—to stop and listen to Jesus's voice—is crucial in the "noise" of today.

—Sally Fesperman, Christian Training Center International, Franklin, North Carolina, United States

✠ ✠ ✠

I first met Noel and Barbara Bell in October 1990, by which time their teaching and lifestyle reflected the precious ministry that we know today as "Sitting at the Feet of Jesus." Their visits to southern Africa formed an important and substantial part of my life. They gathered people together in rich fellowship, teaching from the Word to set apart times to behold, with open faces, the glory of the Lord. Their example of waiting on Jesus has been a blessed encouragement to me and brought me to a place of deeper humility before the King. Through my intimate relationship with the Lord and ongoing guidance, I have had access to many unusual Islamic institutions across Africa, mainly among the rural poor, goat herders, camel drivers and farmers. The Lord has brought the blind from across the Islamic world to my doorstep. The lame and the blind have a special place in Father's strategic heart.

Thank you, Noel and Barbara, for walking in the anointing of your calling.

—Graham Beggs, The King's Trust
(a ministry among the rural poor in South Africa)

✠ ✠ ✠

It was always a great joy to host times of "Sitting at Jesus's Feet" with Noel and Barbara Bell on the island of Åland in Finland. They were rich times of waiting on the Lord and learning to be constantly alert to God's spontaneous initiatives and prophetic words. We are thankful to the Lord for the fellowship we had together in Finland, thankful for how we heard Him speak and how we learned to simply obey Him. Those times have been of great benefit to our current work as missionaries to Colombia and Nepal.

—Antti and Helena Hämäläinen, Åland, Finland

✠ ✠ ✠

After Noel and Barbara first shared the intimate times of "Sitting at the Feet of Jesus," we were prompted to do the same thing in Switzerland; gatherings to sit at His feet have continued ever since. Through experiencing His love and kindness, and His rest and peace, we learned to stop, and listen, and be quiet in His presence. Hearing the whisper of His heart builds me up. Seeing how Jesus works in people's lives while sitting in His presence has produced incredible results. It is essential for all of those who minister in God's kingdom to spend time aside at His feet. His presence protects us from burnout, and opens the way to receive correction from the Master Himself. I love Him so much for who He is. Is there anything greater than His presence?

—Regula Woiwode

When we love someone, we have a deep desire to spend quality time with them. More than anything else, I have a powerful longing to spend time sitting at the feet of Jesus, learning to know His voice and to clearly understand His heart. When I do that during everyday living, it enables me to do His will and not mine. I love Him more than my own life—like my very breath.

—Werner Woiwode,
leaders of Abraham Prayer Ministry, Switzerland

Printed in the United States
By Bookmasters